ROAD TRIP TREASURES
Appalachian Foothills

By D. Jay Powell

Road Trip Treasures
Appalachian Foothills
By D. Jay Powell

About the Cover:
Sunflower photo was provided by Bryan White of
Whitelake Studio and Artful Spaces.
Website: whitelakestudio.com

FOR INFORMATION CONTACT:
D. Jay Powell
P.O. Box 603
Hiram, GA 30141
770-723-6574
Please visit our website at DayTripGetAways.com

Printed in USA

DEDICATION

When the first edition was printed, the book was dedicated to my baby sister, Carol, who had Lou Gehrig's Disease. In actuality, Carol was my wife's youngest sister; however, I adopted her as my own sister. She dealt with this enemy of ALS around 14 years. She inspired many who knew her. Her love for the Lord got her through the battles in this life. Today, she can walk again. Her voice can sing like an angel again. Her arms can hug family members who had been waiting for her. Carol allowed her trouble be used to show the world that there is nothing too hard to get through if one knows the Lord. In 2012, the Lord called her home. I never will forget the stories she would tell. My wife would come home and tell me of Carol's husband waking up in the night, and Carol would be talking clearly. Her husband would say, "Who are you talking to?". She would respond, "The Lord!". She would ask, "Have you come to get me?". The response would be, "Not now, but soon!". While she was at the hospital the last time, we prayed. Our prayer was, "Lord, would you take her, or let her walk out of the hospital." The Lord answered both. She went to sleep and awoke into the presence of Jesus.

CONTENTS

BEFORE YOU BEGIN (HOW TO USE THIS BOOK)

One doesn't have to travel far to find a great getaway. If you have never explored the Southwestern end of the Appalachian foothills, why not? We have some of the most unique treasures not to be found anywhere else.

Planning a trip can be time consuming, regardless if it is for the family, a group at your local church, a school field trip, or business. While this book is not an exhaustive travel guide, Appalachian Foothills - Southwestern Treasures was written to help brainstorm the possibilities.

A variety of ideas are given for every age, taste, and budget. Most of the treasures are convenient to north Georgia and north Alabama. Some are along the way to popular destinations, such as the coast of travelling through the Smokies. A well-planned journey can prevent some of the inconvenience associated with traveling. Some want first-class amenities, while others want a taste of small-town, Southern flavor. Some places are open all day, or the sidewalks roll up at a certain time every day. Some things may be seasonal, or better for certain age groups.

The entries have been shared for information only, so the readers may decide for themselves if they would like to sample some of the unique treasures found along the way. Be sure to check out the contact information provided before setting out on your journey, due to the fact that unexpected changes might have occurred after the writing of this book, or of course the possibility of human error.

Biggest & Best

Featured world records, American wonders, and more Southern favorites

Yes, this sign is on 411 South coming into the Georgia Smokies near Chatsworth.

BIGGEST AND BEST
Featuring world records, American wonders, and more

In the foothills, at the southwestern end of the Appalachian region, are some of the most unusual treasures that will not be found anywhere else. One of the world's largest triplex of underground caverns is located in Georgia, Alabama, and Tennessee. One doesn't have to travel out to the midwest when they can stay in our region to find the footsteps of the Native American Indians or cowboys. America's longest journey into space began here. The longest and deepest lakes, the highest peaks, and abundance of outdoor adventure can be found in our backyard. Athletes from all over the world come to train and compete. So, what is the draw? Discover for yourself!

COMMERCIAL CAVERNS HOLD SIX WORLD RECORDS

Just outside of Huntsville, Alabama, there is a wonder of nature that has been recognized for not only one world record, but six in the Alabama State Park system. It is open year round and welcomes church and school groups to take a tour. Picnic and primitive camping areas are available. Guided tours into the cave are available at a reasonable fee. "Goliath" is the name of the largest known stalagmite in the world and is 45 feet tall. The cave is known for the world's largest stalagmite forest. The cave has the world's flow stone wall. It has the world's largest improbable formation of a stalagmite. It is also known for the world's largest frozen waterfall. The first thing you notice about the Cathedral Caverns is the massive entrance. The huge opening measures 126 feet wide and

25 feet high, and it gets even better! Inside the cavern, you will find Big Rock Canyon, Mystery River, and some of the most beautiful formations God has ever created.

Find out more:
Cathedral Caverns State Park
Woodville, AL
Phone: 256-728-8193

MOST MEMORABLE JOURNEY

Travel 200 miles without leaving northwest Georgia on a journey that could take more than a couple of days. Native Americans settled the Western Hemisphere for thousands of years. Learn how other cultures came to the New World, bringing explorers from Europe and other lands. Newer settlers feared that the Native American culture and theirs could not live safely together. Other pioneers developed a fever that was contagious with greed. They sought to take gold from those who claimed this territory before they came. In fact, it is estimated that some gold was hidden by native ancestors from the earlier explorers and has yet to be found. Discover how they fought on the side of the British, and the militia that would eventually lead to the American Revolution. Learn how they were forced from their lands by those who were too greedy to let them stay as they tried to make peace. The Indians created their own form of government and published a printed newspaper. It is said that the way they were removed was unconstitutional. Because of what they gave up, it's worth taking some time to learn their story. Walk a while in their footsteps. After all, they walked 2200 miles across nine states, and many never made it to their destination.

Find out more:
Native American Tour
Phone: 1-800-733-2280
Website: chieftainstrail.com

SEVEN WONDERS OF AMERICA

Between 1967 and 1973, more than a dozen space rockets were used by NASA's Apollo and Skylab programs. The Saturn V Rocket remains the most powerful machine ever launched. The March Flight Center in Huntsville, Alabama, was the place where the Saturn V was designed under the leadership of Scientist Wernher. This mammoth of a machine was taller than a 36 story building. The fuel required to carry this rocket on a mission would be enough to drive a large family vehicle around the world about 400 times! When it re-entered the earth's atmosphere, it would generate enough electricity to light Los Angeles more than a minute and a half. The spacecraft was assembled using 15 miles of wire. It could reach a height of 50 miles in a few seconds at the rate speed of 6,164 miles per hour. It would burn almost 3,400 gallons of fuel per second. The Davidson Center for Space Exploration houses one of the Saturn V at the Huntsville Space and Rocket Center in Huntsville, Alabama.

Find out more:
Huntsville Space and Rocket Center
Huntsville, AL
Phone: 1-800-63-SPACE
Website: SpaceCamp.com

LONGEST PARK SPANS THE ENTIRE STATE NORTH TO SOUTH

The park opened in 1998 and is 53rd in the Tennessee State Park system. It spans 300 miles between Cumberland Gap National Park in Kentucky and southward near Chattanooga, Tennessee and north Georgia's Chickamauga Battlefield. There are hiking grades at various levels through the eleven counties in Tennessee. See beautiful overlooks, waterfalls, wildlife, and nature undisturbed.

Find out more:
Cumberland Trail Conference
Crossville, TN
Phone: 931-456-6259
Website: Cumerlandtrail.org

LARGEST SOUTHERN MAN MADE LAKE EAST OF THE MISSISSIPPI RIVER

Lake Strom Thurmond was made between the late 1940's and early 1950's and is the 10th most visited of the CORPS lakes in the nation. It was the first USACE Lake on the Savannah River. Millions come to enjoy the lake's amenities from around the country. There are more than 71,000 acres of water and it has shoreline of 1,200 miles.

Find out more:
Lake Strom Thurmond Dam and Lake U.S. Army Corps of Engineers
Clarks Hill, SC
Phone: 1-800-533-3478.

HIGHEST ELEVATION IN THE DEEP SOUTH

From Brasstown Bald, one can see the southwestern region of the Appalachian foothills. As the mountain range of the Carolinas meet northeast Georgia, the elevation height of 4,784 feet at the top of Brasstown Bald overlooks the four states of Georgia, North Carolina, South Carolina, and Tennessee. There is a visitors center, observation deck, hiking trails, and information about the people who once lived in this region for thousands of years. Native Americans who once lived here leave behind a story of a great flood which was survived by those who would climb aboard a giant canoe; all the others died. The canoe rested on the peak of the mountain. The Great Spirit removed a forest to create farmland so the natives could farm until the water receded. This story sounds like it originated from the Biblical story that was handed down over centuries, indicating that someone centuries earlier knew about the worldwide flood.

Find out more:
Blairsville Ranger Office
Blairsville, GA
Phone: 706-745-6928
Additional information available from:
Brasstown Bald Visitors Information Center
Phone: 706-896-2556

SOUTHWESTERN APPALACHIAN MOUNTAIN PEAKS ONE LAST TIME

The range gently meanders across north Alabama and north Mississippi into smaller hills and valleys. Westward, no other brow east of the Mississippi River can claim a higher elevation than Cheaha in the Talladega National Forest. The Alabama State Park system created the Cheaha State Park and Lodge with amenities of scenic views, hiking, swimming, dining, and lodging.

Find out more:
Cheaha State Park Lodge
Delta, AL
Phone: 800-ALA-PARK

NORTH GEORGIA'S LARGEST ANTIQUE MALL

Find collectibles, pottery, china, toys. Coke collectibles, books, jewelry, and more! Enjoy browsing 10,000 square feet and 45 antique dealers. Who knows what treasures you may find? They work hard at keeping a nice place for the customers to shop. Established in 2004, they are working on their sixth year in business.

Find out more:
Hiawassee Antique Mall
Hiawassee, GA
Phone: 706-896-0587
Website: hiawasseeantiquemall.com

LARGEST OUTLET MALL IN NORTHWEST GEORGIA

Calhoun Prime Outlet Mall. You will find these Prime Outlet stores throughout the Southeast. Calhoun is the home to the largest outlet mall in northwest Georgia. Among the selection are fifty brand name outlet stores. They boast of savings up to 65% off suggested retail. Coming through town? Stop by! Conveniently located between Atlanta, Georgia and Chattanooga, Tennessee.

Find out more:
Prime Outlets
Calhoun, GA 30701
Phone: 706-602-1305
Website: PrimeOutlets.com

1996 Olympics

North of McCaysville on Highway 6, the Ocoee Whitewater Center welcomes an average of 300,000 visitors per year. This was the location of the 1996 Olympic canoe, kayak, and slalom events. The Ocoee River is known as a favorite spot for water rafting all over the world. There are educational programs and other events during the year at the 7,200 square foot facility. There are several rafting companies and campgrounds nearby. Also, there are a number of hiking and biking trails, or if you wish, simply find a spot for a picnic or a swim.

Find out more: Ocoee Whitewater Center
Copperhill, TN
Phone: 423-496-0100

MOST SCENIC DRIVE IN NORTH GEORGIA

Take a leisurely drive starting along the west end of this scenic byway route of a 170 mile stretch between Dahlonega and Toccoa, Georgia. While a direct east route across the state would take much less time, charming historic towns, backdrops of mountain scapes and hidden treasures along the way are more in abundance as you head north from Dahlonega toward Blairsville on Route 19. Once in Blairsville, take Route 76 east through the towns of Young Harris and Hiawassee. Continue east on Route 76 east. In Clayton, go south on Route 441 toward the town of Toccoa (off of Route 17). A well-planned journey can make traveling safer in higher elevations through mountain ranges of north Georgia. You will discover side trips in abundance with natural beauty at no additional cost. The number of places to stay and things you will see or do along the way would be too many to mention! Take as much time as you wish. You can't do it all in one trip. Perhaps return to find more reasons folks like you are drawn to north Georgia from all around the country.

Find out more:
Gainesville, GA
Website: georgiamountains.org

MOST UNUSUAL ACCOMPLISHMENTS

Imagine having an opportunity to stand in front of the President and other government officials to give a speech in Washington, DC. Imagine having eyes that could not see the face to whom you were speaking, or making sounds from your voice that were clear to those around you without ever hearing a sound coming from your own lips. Wonder what it would be like to only be able to have all responses interpreted to you by the few who could communicate to a person who is both deaf and blind?

Helen Keller is known around the world and her story begins in a small, rural town in the Appalachian foothills of north Alabama. As an educator, she opened many doors to help many, when most would have given them the title of "hopeless." Born in 1880, she would develop a rare disease that would leave her deaf and blind for the rest of her life. Yet, when someone took the time to communicate with her, she became a beacon of hope for future generations.

Find out more:
Helen Keller Birthplace
300 N. Commons St.
Tuscumbia, AL
Phone: 256-383-4066
Website: helenkellerbirthplace.org

MUST SEE
TRAILS AND TOURS

The pedestrian bridge crossing the river in downtown Rome, Georgia. There are restaurants, shops to browse, a museum, etc.

MUST SEE TRAILS AND TOURS
Featured scenic drives, historic trails, museums and more southern favorites

From many overlooks, one can understand why folks meander through scenic byways in the heart of the South. Why do folks spend hours watching the variety of birds in flight, or enjoy a new section of our rivers and streams from one side of the state to the other over a long period of time? If trails could talk, stories would be told of Spanish explorers looking for buried treasure, footsteps of the Redcoats would be heard from a distance, and the drum beat of Native Americans would be pounding as they echoed against the sky. The militia would be seen as they were defending the American Liberty. Learn about the cost of our brave soldiers to fight so that we could still be free. Meander down a trail that would offer you a glimpse into the past. Discover why folks are drawn to the sounds of music coming from the foothills. Discover why travelers from across the world have found hope in the way we have worshipped for centuries. Take a journey you will not soon forget.

SCENIC AMERICAN BYWAY

The Lookout Mountain Parkway meanders through the three states of Alabama, Georgia, and Tennessee. More than ninety miles of beauty make this path one of the America's "most scenic byways." High peaks, cascading waterfalls, and canyon rims dot the nature scapes that compels visitors to often pass this way. Along the path, discover what makes this region part of the State Park and National Park system. Unique towns, attractions, and getaways are among the treasures to be found between Chattanooga, Tennessee and Gadsden, Alabama.

Find out more:
Dekalb County Tourist Association (Alabama)
Phone: 1-888-805-4740
Website: discoverlookoutmountain.com

SCENIC RIVER TRAIL

This is considered the largest organized river trail meandering through one state. More than 600 miles are mapped, beginning with the Coosa River in northwest Georgia and continuing south to the Gulf of Mexico. Nine lakes and seven rivers offer a variety of adventure for every age and skill level. Lodging and campsites are available to those who travel by sea. Along the way, one can see protected wildlife and historic sites that tell a story all its own. Enjoy the day or make it an extended getaway. Float down the banks of Alabama's scenic rivers. Bring your own boat or rent one from an outfitter along the trail.

Find out more:
Website: alabamascenicrivertrail.com

A TRIP OUT OF THIS WORLD

One of the largest major players in the nation's space program is located in the southwestern foothills of Appalachia in Huntsville, Alabama. Learn about the work of famous rocket scientist Dr. Wernher Von Braun and others. With all the rockets on display, really cool exhibits, and hands-on learning opportunities, time travel becomes a reality. You will discover the space program from its infancy until now as you travel through space. Also, you will see something that has been referred to as one of the seven wonders of America, the Saturn V rocket is housed on location. Find out the U.S. Space and Rocket Center's role in the Apollo mission, the Space Shuttle program, the International Space Station, and more.

Find out more:
Huntsville Space and Rocket Center
Phone: 1-800-63-Space
Website: spacecamp.com

CREATION PLANETARIUM

Watch the night sky and see an amazing journey into God's creation. There are programs for children through adults at Camp Sunrise, as they focus on God's Creation, the Flood, and more. Throughout the year there are events for families and groups. Browse the Creation Museum and discover interesting things about the Great Flood, the days of creation, the planets, comets, the mysterious Solar System, and the Chronology of the Crucifixion.

Find out more:
Camp Sunrise Inc.
Fairmount, GA
Phone: 706-337-2775
Website: campsunrise.com

BLUE AND GRAY TRAIL

Appomattox, Virginia, tells of some of the final moments of the Civil War. Georgia follows in the footsteps of the Confederate and Union Army, telling the story that led to the end. After the Battle of Chickamauga, the only battle with more casualties would be at Gettysburg as brother fought against brother. By the time of the "March to the Sea," the South would be left in ruins. Within the rural small towns, there are stories left behind of those whose families survived as their own farms and towns were turned into battlefields that we one day would call home.

Find out more:
Website: BlueandGrayTrail.com

LITTLE RIVER CANYON NATIONAL PRESERVE

Little River Canyon National Preserve has been listed as a part of the National park system since 1992. Winding roads and scenic vistas atop Lookout Mountain near Fort Payne, Alabama, make this scenic drive popular to photographers of every age. This canyon is one of the deepest gorges east of the Mississippi River, with the depth of about 700 feet. Enjoy unique wildlife, see high waterfalls, and find the perfect picnic spot. It's convenient to swimming and hiking.

Find out more:
Little River Canyon National Preserve
4322 Little River Trail NE
Suite 100
Fort Payne, AL 35967
Phone: 256-845-9605

ONE OF AMERICA'S LARGEST BATTLEFIELDS

After the Civil War, the Chickamauga and Chattanooga Battlefields became a national landmark that draws thousands of visitors per year and has been preserved for generations to come. It would become the bloodiest two days of September 1863. Close to 20,000 infantry were lost on the Confederate's side, while the Union Army lost more than 15,000 men. Take a guided tour or self guided walk through the grounds. See various memorials. The sizes themselves tell an important piece of historical information. Enter the museum for a glance of the men in uniform and the weapons they used.

Find out more:
Chickamauga and Chattanooga National Battlefield Park
Fort Oglethorpe, GA
Phone: 706-866-9241
Website: nps.gov/chch

VISIT THE NATION'S CAPITOL

By the 1800s, there was a determination by some who wanted the total removal of the Native Americans from this region. By the mid 1820s a constitution, a government model, was adopted similar to the United States, to show they could dwell peacefully. In what is now Gordon County, Georgia, the Native Americans created a village that would become their nation's capitol. History leaves ruins of their past of the government buildings, farms, trading post, a school, a church, and a newspaper called The Cherokee Phoenix. It is still being published today on a reservation. One of the only original structures still standing is the missionary's home. By the late 1830s they were locked up until they were marched westward on what is referred to as the Trail of Tears. Come walk the village and learn about their story.

Find out more:
New Echota State Historic Site
Calhoun, GA
Phone: 706-624-1321

THE AMERICAN VILLAGE

The setting is during the Colonial era, and the founding of a new nation is the goal. Bring a group and your imagination to experience the days of the American Revolution. Step back in time and be a part of history as it comes to life. Who know what notable Americans you may see or even meet during your visit, from presidents to statesmen, or even the militia who fought to preserve what freedoms we have today. The buildings, the people, and their way of life will perhaps make you forget for a moment that you're not living in the 1700s.

Find out more:
The American Village
3727 Highway 119 S.
Montevallo, AL
Phone: 205-665-3535
Website: Americanvillage.org

NORTH ALABAMA HALLELUJAH TRAIL

In the South, we take refuge in our worship, regardless of the denominational ties. Since the nation's beginning, this has been a Divine gift that has been a part of the very fabric of our lives. Praise to our Lord, prayer upon our hearts, and guidance from the Holy Scriptures are shared with the fellowship of those who hold dear the same convictions. Each sanctuary was built beautifully with well-designed architecture, or with the simplicity of humble beginnings. Today, many of the 32 churches are more than 100 years old, still holding services across a sixteen county region in north Alabama.

Find out more:
Alabama Mountain Lakes Tourist Association
Phone: 1-800-648-5381
Website: northalabama.org

COURTHOUSE TRAIL

Travel the Martha Berry Highway north to south, and discover for yourself some of the nation's most historic structures. More than twenty districts on a 345 mile stretch tell their own story. Learn of the architecture that was influenced by cultures from around the world whose foundations date back more than 100 years. From the top of the state to the nearby coastal towns, many are within reach. Take one day at a time, spend a few days with your camera in hand along the west side of Georgia exploring the Courthouse Trail.

Find out more:
Along the Martha Berry Highway
Website: Hwy 27.com

SIXTH CAVALRY MUSEUM

The heroes of a nation at war can be found in the Sixth U.S. Cavalry. Organized around the time of the Civil War, they fought at Williamsburg and Gettysburg. They were also involved in the Indian Wars, Spanish American War with Teddy Roosevelt and the Rough Riders. You will soon discover how they were involved in World War I and World War II.

Find out more:
Sixth Cavalry Museum
Fort Oglethorpe, GA
Phone: 706-861-2860
Website: 6thcavalrymuseum.org

NORTH ALABAMA RAILROAD MUSEUM

Discover the North Alabama Railroad Museum near Huntsville, Alabama. Learn about the history and how they are preserving the memory of the railroad. Take a self-guided tour, or request a guided tour for a side of the tracks you may not otherwise experience. Perhaps you will share their love of trains as kids of every age see several types of cars and locomotives onsite. See the nation's smallest union depot. Some of the highlights of your visit include an opportunity to see a post office car, a Pullman sleeper, and a 1914 diner car.

Find out more:
North Alabama Railroad Museum
Near Huntsville
Phone: 256-851-6276
Website: northalabamarailroadmuseum.com

HEART OF DIXIE RAILROAD MUSEUM

South of Birmingham, Alabama, you will realize why it is referred to as the "official railroad museum of the state." Use the library, browse the collection of artifacts, see a variety of railroad cars, and restored depots. Learn about the rich history of the railroad.

Find out more:
Heart of Dixie Railroad Museum
Caleria, AL
Phone: 205-668-3435
Website: hodrm.org

SOUTHERN RAILWAY MUSEUM

Some of the cars are more than 100 years old, and there are almost 100 cars on location. Everyone likes cabooses, and there are several to choose from. See a variety of old fashioned locomotives and diesel engines. Passenger cars, diner cars, freight cars, and baggage cars are among the selection on this 35-acre site. Whatever the reason, you will want to plan a trip to the Georgia Southern Railway Museum in Duluth, Georgia.

Find out more:
Phone: 770-476-2013
Website: srmduluth.org

NORTH ALABAMA BIRDING TRAIL

Almost 400 types of birds have been seen across the Yellowhammer State. Watch a bald eagle in flight. Clock a sandpiper traveling speeds greater than 100 miles an hour. See a white pelican with a wingspan of about nine feet. Look for a ruby throated hummingbird that is one of the most common in this part of the foothills. There are fifty great sites across north Alabama for photographers of every age. So bring your camera and every picture includes a scenic backdrop at no additional charge!

Website: alabamabirdingtrails.com

ROUTE 61 ROAD TOUR

More than you can do in a day! This path begins in the downtown historic district of Cartersville, Georgia and meanders south through Dallas and Villa Rica. One will find a sample of small town America at its best! Tour museums, bring a bike or rent one and spend the day on a ninety mile stretch across an old rail line. Really cool walking tours and driving tours are available. Visit historic churches and walk in the footsteps of evangelist Sam Jones, China missionary Lottie Moon, and gospel music writer Thomas Dorsey. Discover the Civil War battles that took place and the Union Army lost. Cross the paths of the

Native Americans who once roamed these parts. Browse many unique shops within a seven county region. Sample a taste of dining that has been a staple to the locals for years.

Find out more:
Phone: 770-723-6574
Website: DayTripGetAways.com

Adventure Excursions

Featured railways, marinas, caving, flying, biking, and more Southern favorites.

Scenic view from Mentone, Alabama just off the Lookout Mountain Parkway.

ADVENTURE EXCURSIONS
Featuring biking, boating, marinas, railway, caving, flying, and more.

Millions of folks travel through the southwestern end of the Appalachian region each year where there is an abundance of adventure around every turn. For those who stay, they find an outdoor lover's paradise! There are a wide variety of outdoor sports from rock climbing, hang-gliding, canoeing, spelunking, horseback riding, skiing, hiking, biking, flying, ballooning, mazing, and the list continues. There are things for every outdoor enthusiast of every age and at every level of experience. Some things are seasonal, while other attractions are year round. So, church groups can plan their next retreat, school groups can schedule an adventure trip, or businesses can offer a team building excursion. Perhaps moms and dads can take the family on a trip suited for them. Whatever the reason, have a blast this season unlike any other place in the country.

ROAMING DOWN THE RIVER

Get a taste of adventure as you venture down the river along the Coosa and other tributaries. The Coosa River Basin Initiative is a non-profit organization based in Rome, Georgia that provides recreational trips from our north Georgia rivers at a very reasonable price. Their focus is to provide education and help protect our waterways as millions of gallons are used every day, creating thousands of jobs and drinking water for thousands of folks living in our region. Getting involved can be a fun way to help the environment as you help make the rivers and streams clean and safe.

Find out more:
Coosa River Basin Initiative
Rome, GA 30161
Phone: 706-232-2724
Website: Coosa.org

SILVER COMET TRAIL AND CHIEF LADIGA TRAIL

People travel from all over the country to ride these trails. There are some bike rentals available. Check out the biking opportunities along the Silver Comet Trail and the Chief Ladiga Trail. There is a ninety-mile stretch between Smyrna, Georgia and Anniston, Alabama. This was an old train trestle that has made a great bike path. It is fun, safe, and better to travel in groups. You will want to plan your bike excursion ahead to see where trail access is limited due to weather and other factors.

Find out more:
Website: PathFoundation.org and Chiefladiga.com

BLUE RIDGE SCENIC RAILWAY
Venture on a railroad excursion for a trip that you will not soon forget along the historic Toccoa River. Once you cross the Tennessee line, it becomes the Ocoee River. Have fun taking the train ride that begins in Blue Ridge, Georgia and arrives in McCaysville. Enjoy one of their rafting and rail combos. Participants combine a train ride with a rafting adventure, or leisurely tubing down the river.

Find out more:
Blue Ridge, GA 30513
Phone: 877-413-8724
Website: brscenic.com

WORLD'S LARGEST MAZE - RESACA, GEORGIA

Can you find the way out of this puzzle? From September through November, go on an adventure through one of the world's largest corn mazes. See if you can figure your way out of the thirty acres, Cagle's Dairy cuts a path open to the public during the fall that's for the whole family. You will want to check out their hayrides, weenie roasts, and special events, and the nights they are open late at the maze.

Find out more:
Cagle's Dairy Farm
Resaca, GA
Phone: 770-345-5591

HIKE BRASSTOWN BALD

Great exercise if you can take the hill! Bring your family, church group, or a school group. Take a steep hike to the top of Brasstown Bald. This is the highest peak in Georgia. At the top, there is a 360-degree observation deck, overlooking four states on a clear day. You will climb 500 feet in a half-mile to the top that is 4,784 feet above sea level. The views are spectacular. There is a museum inside the Visitors Center where you can learn about the people of the area.

Find out more:
Blairsville Rangers Office
1881 Highway 515
Blairsville, GA 30512
Phone: 706-745-6928
Website: n-georgia.com

HORSEBACK RIDING: TASTE OF THE MIDWEST WITHOUT LEAVING THE SOUTHEAST

Stay on the ranch and go on a horseback riding adventure in the beautiful Sequatchie Valley. There is only one other one like it in the entire world on the continent of Africa. The Valley is 100 miles long and five miles wide. This hidden treasure is outside of Chattanooga in Dunlap, Tennessee. This is an excellent excursion to plan for church groups. Plan to stay over for the excursion to plan for church groups. Plan to stay over for the weekend and ride to church on horseback! Great way to celebrate anniversaries, birthdays, and other special occasions.

Find out more:
Sequatchie Valley Guest Ranch
Phone: 423-554-4677
Website: tnhorsevacation.com

OCOEE WHITEWATER CENTER

Professional athletes have come here from all over the world. The Ocoee Whitewater Center was built for the 1996 Olympics canoe, kayak, and slalom competitions.

The Ocoee has been one of the most popular venues for whitewater rivers for years, and became an obvious choice for the events the year the competitions came to Atlanta. Today, the OWWC receives 300,000 visitors annually because of the variety of activities. While a rafting adventure is the most popular choice of activities, there is biking and hiking at the center for the outdoor enthusiast. The information to plan your trip is listed for your convenience. Check out the list of companies that provide services for the Hiawassee and Ocoee Rivers. They can help you plan your excursion with regard to the season and restrictions on the rivers.

Find out more:
Ocoee Whitewater Center
Copperhill, TN 37317
Phone: 423-496-0100

CARTERS LAKE MARINA

North Georgia has a best kept secret in recreational activities. Enjoy one of the largest lakes in the state of Georgia. Carters Lake Marina has houseboats and pontoon boats for rental. Lake-side cabins are also available. There is something for every budget. Take advantage of the amenities of the lake while at the marina to add to your adventure!

Find out more:
Carters Lake Marina and Resort
Chatsworth, GA 30705
Phone: 706-276-4891
Website: CartersLake.com

CHATTANOOGA TRAIN EXCURSION

Select a variety of trips lasting from sixty minutes to six hours, depending upon how much time you have to spare. A number of special packages are offered throughout the year. If you have a group large enough, groups may charter a special riding event for the organization. For a dynamic railway adventure, consider one of the many trips out of Chattanooga. Take a journey around Missionary Ridge or down the tracks across northwest Georgia to Chickamauga. Charter trips are fun for everyone. While you are in Chattanooga, check out the museum and learn of their railroad history.

Find out more:
Tennessee Valley Railroad Museum
Chattanooga, TN
Phone: 423-894-8028
Website: tvrail.com

TREE CANOPY TOURS

Take a trip through the treetops! This attraction has been featured on WSB-TV. It is truly a hidden attraction in Georgia. The zip line is one of the largest of its kind in the United States. Choose what you want to try. Trip can last from an hour to five hours, depending on the course. Some places are more than 100 feet above the ground and a half mile long. Ask about the overnight packages while you are enjoying the Tree Canopy Tour.

Find out more:
Historic Banning Mills

Whitesburg, GA
Phone: 770-834-9149
Website: historicbanningmills.com

Southern Inspirations

Historic Churches, Historic Sites, Productions, and more!

Evangelist Sam Jones Pastored Old Van Wert Church, Rockmart, Georgia.

SOUTHERN INSPIRATIONS
Featured historic churches, heritage sites, hymns, productions, and more!

Venture back to an era when the Western Hemisphere was a fertile mission field. Learn how some of the early pioneers were arrested for their continued service to the Native Americans that were forced to march west. Climb the world's largest Ten Commandments. Stay at one of America's featured Christian retreats. Discover some of the country's oldest churches. Tour the home of a President. Take a tour of an old settlement of a group who were exiled to the New World. Learn how a Sunday school was the birthplace of the world's largest college campus. Sing hymns that began in our own backyard. Discover an American heritage that has inspired millions to come worship the way we do in the Bible belt!

BIBLES TO THE CHEROKEE

The evangelization of the Cherokee became the goal of the American Mission Board during the early 1800s. One of the settlements, which was created in 1823 and was called Wills Town, is today Fort Payne, Alabama. There is a marker that tells of the community that once thrived. A few miles away one can find what is left of the mission and cemetery marking the site. It was here the Cherokee alphabet was created a few years prior, allowing Christian missionaries to translate the Bible into Cherokee language. The mission remained active until 1838, when the Cherokee were stockaded by the federal government and marched west in what became known as the "Trail of Tears." Fort Payne is named after the fort that was built to stockade the Indians and the officer, Major John Payne, who was in charge of the move west.

Find out more:
Marker is located in park downtown Fort Payne

WORLD'S LARGEST TEN COMMANDMENTS

Not too far from the Tennessee state line in Murphy, South Carolina, is a landmark that is referred to as the largest kind, as it stretches across a mountainside. More than 300 steps will take you to the top, or you can drive. The letters are five feet tall. There are some other things to see, such as a large cross and a replica of Christ's tomb.

Find out more:
Fields of the Woods
Phone: 828-494-7855
Website: Fieldsofthewoodbiblepark.com

A MOUNTAIN RETREAT

Billy Graham Training Center at The Cove is a Christian mountain retreat nestled in the mountains of Asheville, North Carolina. Folks are welcome to come by regular business hours to relax and enjoy breathtaking view of the Smoky Mountains. There are opportunities to attend events and conferences from nationally known Christian speakers, if registered in advance, or stay overnight in one of the lodging facilities. There is a dining room and other amenities. The main purpose is to provide a place where God's people can come, study the Word of God, and pray.

Find out more:
The Cove
Asheville, NC
Phone: 828-298-2092
Website: thecove.org

BOY PRESIDENT

Woodrow Wilson lived in the historic town of Augusta,
Georgia as a boy, longer than any other as he grew up. He
was a son of a Presbyterian minister. Next door lived
another minister whose son became a Supreme Court
Justice. Woodrow Wilson was born in Staunton, Virginia.
As an adult, he became Governor of New Jersey before
becoming President of the United States. However, it was
in this home in Augusta where his leadership and strong
Christian faith were developed.

Find out more:
Woodrow Wilson Boyhood Home
Phone: 706-722-9828
Website: wilsonboyhoodhome.org

THIRD OLDEST CHURCH

First Presbyterian Church, the oldest Presbyterian church
in Augusta, Georgia, was where the Presbyterian Church
in the United States was formed. It was a Christian
denomination from 1861 to 1963 until it merged with
another Presbyterian denomination. The architect who
drew the plans for the original structure actually was the

first native-born designer in America. He was also responsible for creating the plans for the Washington Monument. This church is the 23rd oldest in the nation and the third in the state of Georgia in its denomination. President Woodrow Wilson's father was the pastor of Augusta's First Presbyterian Church and founder of the newly established PCUS.

Find out more:
First Presbyterian Church
Augusta, GA

EARLY SETTLEMENT

This 250-year-old German Protestant settlement has become a national landmark. During the French and Indian Wars, this was a French fort as well. Learn the way they lived and worshipped. There is a visitors center. The restored church dates back to 1788 after the American Revolution. There is a reconstructed village and French fort. See tour guides and living history in dress of the day. Pioneers built the first Moravian settlement in North Carolina here at Bethabara Park. Check out the amenities and special events.

Find out more:
Historic Bethabara Park
Winston-Salem, NC
Phone: 336-924-8191

EXILED TO COLONIAL AMERICA

This group of Lutheran settlers came from Salzburg, Austria and settled along the Savannah River and created the town of New Ebenezer during 1736. An orphanage that was founded in Germany in 1698 continued in this settlement. They established the first Sunday school. The Jerusalem Evangelical Lutheran Church was built in 1741, making it the oldest congregation in the state. Georgia's first Governor came from this settlement. Tour the museum on site.

Find out more:
Georgia Salzburger Society
Georgia Highway 275
Rincon, GA
Phone: 912-754-7001
Website: visitebenezer.com

FROM A LITTLE SUNDAY SCHOOL

Martha Berry has been recognized as a pioneer in education. She began her journey in the late 1800s when she realized local children did not know the Bible, nor could they read. So she began a Sunday school class to share with them the truth of the Word of God. From this seed that had been planted came the need to open her first school to provide a quality education. Tour the historic sites at Berry College in Floyd County, Georgia to learn how the school became known as the world's largest campus.

Find out More:
Berry College
Martha Berry Highway
Mount Berry, GA
Phone: 706-232-5374
Website: berry.edu

GRAND OLE OPRY

Former home of Nashville's Grand Ole Opry has historic roots in the path of evangelism that swept the nation in the last part of the 18th century. Thomas Ryman came to faith in Jesus Christ after a revival preached by the well known evangelist of the day, Sam Jones. He lived in Cartersville, Georgia and was a preacher of the Van Wert circuit. Thomas Ryman built the Union Gospel Tabernacle in 1892 so the evangelist would have a place to preach when he came to Nashville. Later the facility became known as the Ryman Auditorium. Reservations can be made to tour this national landmark.

Find out more:
Ryman Auditorium
Nashville, TN 37219
Phone: 615-458-8700

TOUR LITTLE JERUSALEM

In the heart of the Southeast, tour a city that is known around the world as "Jerusalem in Miniature." Sculpted with the smallest detail and taking decades to complete by one man who worked tirelessly at the monastery with his regular duties. Take a tour of the Holy Land in Miniature and see this masterpiece unveiled as you walk among more than 100 replicas of places around the world in this four acre park. See Rome, the Great Wall of China, the Hanging Gardens of Babylon, Jerusalem, and other ancient pieces.

Find out more:
St. Bernard Retreat & Conference Center
Cullman, AL 35055
Phone: 256-734-4110
Website: avermariagrotto.com

CRADLE OF EVANGELISM

Shubert Sterns and Daniel Marshall were brothers-in-law and preachers who worked consistently together in evangelism from 1754 until 1771 when Sterns passed away. That same year, Daniel Marshall pastored the Kiokee Baptist Church of Appling and is considered to be the oldest Baptist church in Georgia near Augusta. Out of this church came the Georgia Baptist Convention and later the Southern Baptist Convention. However, Shubert Sterns had begun the first work in the South of the two preachers in 1755 after moving from Virginia to the area today known as Randolph County, North Carolina. He started the Sandy Creek Baptist Church while continuing his preaching ministry. One of the structures is still standing as a historic landmark. The two men never realized what would come from their work, since it sprouted after they passed away. Since this was the first seed planted of their work in the South, it is referred to by some as the "Mother of the Southern Baptist Convention."

Find out more:
Visitor information
Liberty, NC 27298
Phone: 800-626-2672

THE DAWN OF A GREAT AWAKENING

Great Britain and Spain sought control of the southeastern part of the New World. James Oglethorpe was sent to establish a new colony near Savannah in 1733 to defend the other colonies against the Spanish who had settled in Florida. On board the ship of the 275 passengers were two famous brothers, John and Charles Wesley. Once they arrived, there was a fort established on St. Simons Island. The Wesley brothers established a church that today is called Christ Church. George Whitfield ministered there for a period when he came from Europe. Take a guided tour or self-guided tour in their footsteps on St. Simons Island, Georgia.

VAN WERT CHURCH

The rural town of Rockmart, Georgia preserves a historic church to tell a story of a community that once thrived. This would be the first church pastored by one of America's famous evangelists of the late 1800s, Sam Jones. This small church has been the worship place of several mainstream denominations in the heart of the Bible belt.

NEW ECHOTA

Native American missions became a focus for missionary agencies during the colonial years of a younger nation. With the invention of the Cherokee alphabet, the task became easier to work among the Indians. New Echota became the last capital of the Cherokee in the 1820s. Moravian missionaries lived in the settlement and taught school to the children. The only original structure is the missionary's house in the village. This settlement had updated farms, a trading post, and government facilities of the day. When the Native Americans were moved west, it became illegal to work among them. All missionary efforts had to cease. Some spent time in jail for disobeying the law.
Find out more:
New Echota State Historic Site (Park)
Calhoun, GA
Phone: 706-624-1321

PRECIOUS LORD, TAKE MY HAND

Thomas Dorsey was born in Villa Rica, Georgia in 1899. He would become a music legend of his day. As his career grew, the name "Father of Gospel Music" became a staple. He has been inducted in the Georgia Music Hall of Fame and Nashville Music Hall of Fame. The Thomas Dorsey Gospel Music Festival is held annually in June at the Mt. Prospect Baptist Church in Villa Rica. Thomas Dorsey is known for writing the hymn, "Precious Lord, Take My Hand" after losing his wife during childbirth in 1832. No wonder the song has touched so many lives for almost 90 years.

LIGHT SHOWS AT DESOTO CAVERNS

The cool temperatures at DeSoto Caverns make a great year round destination for families, church groups, and school groups. One of the highlights of the tour are the light shows. See the birth of Christ at Christmas and the Resurrection at Easter. In June and July, they celebrate Independence Day with the "God and Country" light show. Throughout the year they tell the creation story.

Find out more:
DeSoto Caverns Park
Childersburg, AL
Phone: 1-800-933-2283
Website: desotocavernspark.com

LIVE BIBLICAL PRODUCTIONS

Since 1996, the production company has become an attraction to folks through South Carolina to watch the Bible come alive. The calendar is filled with professional shows telling the scenes as given in the Old Testament and New Testament. See the miracles of Jesus. Experience the first Christmas. Watch the Easter story unfold. Plan to come to one of the dinner shows for a journey of a lifetime during one of these quality productions.

Find out more:
NarroWay Productions
Fort Mill, SC
Phone: 803-802-2300
Website: Narroway.net

LEANING ON THE EVERLASTING ARMS

The old stone church in Ringgold was built around 1850 and now has a museum with a lot of information about the area. There is a popular hymn that was sung here for the first time, "Leaning on the Everlasting Arms." This little church also became a hospital for both the Union and Confederate Armies during the Battle of Ringgold as the Civil War made its way through Georgia.

Find out more:
Old Stone Church
Ringgold, GA
Website: cityofringgold.com

EVANGELIST SAM JONES

During the late 1800s, Sam Jones was one of the most popular evangelists of his day. He preached across the country until he passed away in 1906, with 30,000 coming to Atlanta for the service. He pastored in the Van Wert circuit before he went full time as an evangelist. Today, his home in Cartersville, Georgia has a museum where you can learn about his life.

Find out more:
Roselawn
Cartersville, GA
Phone: 770-387-5162
Website: roselawnmuseum.com

NORTH ALABAMA HISTORIC CHURCH TRAIL

More than thirty churches dot the landscape across the North Alabama Lakes region, which spans about 100 years. See beautiful stained glass, wooden pioneer structures, high steeples, and learn some of the history of these churches. Some have elaborate architectural design, while others are simple structures built by those who desired to have a place to worship. They all represent the heart of those who desired to build a place of prayer, worship, to learn the truths for the Scriptures, and for fellowship.

Find out more:
North Alabama Hallelujah Trail
Phone: 800-648-5381
Website: northalabama.org

VISIT THE HOLY LAND

Drive to the Holy Land without leaving the southeastern United States! See replicas of an ancient culture that would bring the world the Holy Bible and last through the sands of time. The Explorations of Antiquity Living History Museum makes the Old Testament and New Testament come to life. Take a trip along the journey of Abraham. Walk ancient streets of Jerusalem in the footsteps of Jesus, from the virgin birth to the Crucifixion and the empty tomb. Visit the times of the Romans, the ancient synagogues, and the catacombs of the first century Christians. Attend a Passover meal. Discover how they lived, worked, and worshipped in the first century. Learn what it must have been like to hear Jesus teach the

Beatitudes, walk on the Sea of Galilee, or raise the dead. There are a number of events throughout the year that will bring the Bible to life!

Find out more:
Explorations in Antiquity Center
LaGrange, GA 30240
Phone: 706-885-0363
Website: explorationsinantiquity.net

Make a Difference

Featuring Volunteering in the Southwestern Appalachian Region

Many opportunities to be a volunteer are endless.

GREAT LAKES ACROSS THE SOUTHEAST

Millions of visitors are drawn to the miles of shoreline opportunities across the country, managed by the United States Army Corp of Engineers. While building our canals, dams, and managing our rivers and streams, they are the nation's largest provider of recreation. Fishing, boating, swimming, and camping are among the many activities. There are many fun and rewarding opportunities offered through their volunteer program. There are a variety of special activities to choose from throughout the year. Some help keep our lakes and streams clean, work at their visitors centers, help build wildlife habitats, or be a tour guide of the dam sites. The next time you take a picnic to one of the great lakes near you, think of ways you can take some time to help!

Find out more:
Website: corpslakes.us

ALABAMA WILDLIFE CENTER

Alabama has some great state parks! Inside Oak Mountain, one will discover a gem that may be for you to discover. This is the oldest wildlife refuge in Alabama. Since 1977, they have helped meet the needs of endangered birds, reptiles, and a variety of 50,000 wildlife species. They need help from volunteers to assist with a number of tasks to run this privately owned, not-for-profit organization. One may assist in providing care for eagles, owls, alligators, turtles, and cougars, to name a few.

Find out more:
Alabama Wildlife Center, Oak Mountain State Park
100 Terrace Drive
Pelham, AL 35124
Phone: 205-663-7930
Website: awrc.org

GET INTO SHOW BUSINESS

Whoever said you were too old? This idea is fun for
everyone and every age. Individuals and groups of
different sizes can be an important part of working with the
celebrities in the community. Who knows, you may
become one! Perhaps you enjoy being in the spotlight on
the stage. Maybe you like doing things behind the scenes
while being up close where the action is. Build a set, use
your artistic ability to paint the backdrop, or help with
setting up props during the big production. Work at the
front entrance and collect the tickets at the box office.
Assist guests to their seats. Help with the clean up. Give
technical support. This is a fun and educational way to use
your skills as a volunteer at your local community theater.

HELP A CHILD

Our children are our leaders of tomorrow. We have to build
the bridge to the future. Find resources that can help you
find opportunities in your own area. Children become
innocent victims of circumstances beyond their control.
Take a moment and make a difference in the lives of our
youth. A few moments of your time make a world of
difference. You may be their only help.

Find out more:
Website: charityguide.org

FRIENDS OF GEORGIA STATE PARKS

Almost fifty chapters of this organization span the state in every direction. Take a ride through the breathtaking mountain scapes or meander through middle Georgia. Walk in the footsteps of the Presidents or signers of the Declaration of Independence. Visit the coast and step back to the Colonial era. Have fun while you're making family memories. Work on a project with your church group. Help preserve our protected preserves, parks, and historic sites.

Find out more: Friendsofgeorgiastateparks.org

NEW PROGRAM AT THE BEAUTIFUL ALABAMA STATE PARKS

The state of Alabama has recently created a new program to give volunteers opportunities across the region. The highest point is near I-20 near the Georgia line at Cheaha. As the Spanish explorer, DeSoto, entered north Alabama as he made his way through Rome, Georgia, the Coosa River would have been one of his routes of transportation. He found a region that would eventually bear his name in the Alabama State Park System. DeSoto Falls State Park Lodge is a nice place to take the load off your feet. Stay on Wheeler Lake that feeds from the Tennessee River. Plan to go south for a few days to visit their Gulf State Park

Lodge. But first, check out the volunteer program. You may like what you hear and keep Alabama parks beautiful!

Find out more:
Phone: 800-Ala-Park
Website: OutDoorAlabama.com
Website: alapark.com/VIP

DOWN THE RIVER

Learn water safety as you kayak or canoe down the river. Paddle on an adventure trip! Help keep the rivers clean. Discover some of the history of the people who used the river as the main pathway between major trading posts. There are a variety of opportunities for different skill levels, and it's probably the best deal around the state. Opportunities may take you where the rivers flow, across Alabama, along the Florida coast, or in your own backyard!

Find out more:
Website: Gapaddle.com

GO CYCLING
One of the nation's best organized bike organizations within a seven state region united to create one of the best bike trail routes for the communities to enjoy. Each group has regular meetings to manage a variety of trails. So bring your bike and enjoy the day! Check out the events, workdays, and information on how to start. Find the closest chapter near you and get cycling!

Find out more:
Website: sorba.org

HELP WITH HEALING

With the number of folks in the hospitals, nursing homes, and Hospice care, families become burdened with taking care of their family members without much of a break. Often there are not enough staff at the facility to meet every need of the patients, regardless of the intentions. There are a number of opportunities volunteers can assist with that can make the day flow a little easier for all involved. For patients whose family never comes for a visit, yours is a blessing in disguise! Check out your local medical facility to see how you can be involved, especially with long-term or terminally ill patients.

CAMP

Church camps and not-for-profit camps are often overlooked until the next summer. There are a number of maintenance issues that need attention and often there is enough funding to take care of all that could be done. Give back to ministries and other organizations by donating your time to assist with getting the camp ready for the next season. Find local camps in your area, take a group, and adopt a project for a worthwhile cause. There are many great ideas for church youth groups and retired folks who may have more free time than most. Let's go camping!

IF YOU LIKE RESEARCH

The Department of Natural Resources often needs volunteers with the assistance of different groups to perform certain tasks relating to historic preservation, from archeological digs to cemetery maintenance across the state. There are a variety of opportunities that you find an interest in as you plan your volunteer calendar.

Find out more:
Website: Gashpo.org

PARTNER IN EDUCATION

Regardless if schools are private, public, or homeschool networks, they are always looking for volunteers to assist with students. There are also a variety of tasks that would not be done without the aid of volunteers. Take some time to read to a child, assist in a classroom, help in the lunchroom, work in the office, help design a bulletin board, and more. Be a partner in education by donating your time during the school year. Helping with tomorrow's future is only a phone call away!

RIDE THE TRAIN

Here is an idea that will keep you on the right track! Check out the opportunity at northwest Georgia's railroad excursion train. It's fun as you assist guests along the banks of the Toccoa River between the Georgia towns of Blue Ridge and McCaysville. While you are there, enjoy the beauty of the north Georgia mountains. Browse quaint shops. Dine at one of the local restaurants flavored with old-fashioned cooking and southern hospitality, so get aboard!

Find out more:
Blue Ridge Scenic Railway
Blue Ridge, GA
Phone: 877-413-8724
Website: brscenic.com

ON THE BATTLEFIELD

Be a part of history as you volunteer to participate in one of the nation's growing interests. With safety as a priority, folks at every age can find ways to participate. Discover through the eyes of those who experienced the Civil War. As cannons blast in the distance, camp out with a regiment in the wilderness as they plan their next course of action. Ride a horse through the forest where a soldier from the other side could approach unexpectedly. Farmers' land became the battleground. Congregations saw their churches burned. Homes became hospitals and headquarters of the military. Dress in clothes of that era. Decide if you want to be on the side of the Union or Confederate Army! Learn how to get started.

Find out more:
Website: reenactmenthq.com

HELP A SENIOR CITIZEN

Since the baby-boomer generation of the post-World War II era have reached retirement age, many opportunities have exploded for you to assist the elderly. Check with your local county organizations, nursing homes, and senior care homes to see how you can be of service. Don't forget parents, grandparents, or senior adults in your own family!

Grand Slam Getaway

Featured major league affiliate teams across the South

Roadside attraction: Mushroom Rock creates a natural entrance to the spectacular Little River Canyon along the Lookout Mountain Parkway.

GRAND SLAM GETAWAYS
Featured Major League Affiliate Teams Across the South

Around the southeastern United States, some of the nation's major leagues are less than a few hour's drive away. From the Atlanta Braves to the New York Yankees, or the Arizona Diamondbacks to the Chicago Cubs, your favorite team may be found in this region. From coast to coast, make it a home run event! They are represented by the affiliations of the minor league clubs in large cities and rural towns. The backdrop of mountain scapes, along the banks of rivers, near the coast, and a variety of natural settings add to the fun of the trip.

History has been made in the fields where Hall of Famers got their start as rookies. Some clubs began when the nation was barely a century old and tell the story of an American pastime that will probably last into the future. Who knows the possibilities? Some may have tours to take you into the past that tell stories of athletes who waited in the dugouts, pitched the fast balls, or who eventually made it to the pros across the nation. If a club changes hands to another major league team from the time this book is written, there will be more stories to write about in the journals of baseball. The few listed are only a sample found in Georgia, Alabama, Tennessee, the Carolinas, and Florida. So, get out your map, set your calendar, and make plans to watch the next future baseball legends being made in the part of the country known for its southern hospitality.

HOW ABOUT THOSE WHITE SOX?

Twenty years after the Civil War, this historic team got its start playing in different ball leagues of the South. Over the decades, the team would be known for its milestones of perfect pitches, bats, and plays that would hit the record books in the minor leagues. Many would recognize the names of some of the professional athletes who wore the Baron uniform, such as Reggie Jackson, Willie Mays, and even Michael Jordan. The Birmingham Barons marked its quarter of a century affiliation with the Chicago White Sox in the 2011 season. More than 250,000 fans have been known to flock to the stands to watch them play.

Find out more:
Birmingham Barons
Birmingham, AL
Phone: 205-988-3200
Website: barons.com

NEW YORK METS

Travel to the Big Apple and don't forget to see the New York Mets! But, if you're in the South, take a trip to Georgia's coast and watch the minor league team, the Savannah Sand Gnats. See where names like Hank Aaron, Babe Ruth, Mickey Mantle, and Jackie Robinson played ball at the historic Grayson Stadium. The New York Mets' affiliation began with the 2007 season. Plan some time in Savannah and include a game on your itinerary.

Find out more:
Savannah Sand Gnats
Savannah, GA
Phone: 912-351-9150
Website: sandgnats.com

ARIZONA DIAMONDBACKS

Who said you had to go to the Sonoran to watch ball in the desert? This minor league team brings western ball to the Southeast in 2007 at the Alabama coast. Fans will keep their eyes on the ball as this team competes across the region over the next few years. So, if you can take the heat, make a trip to the beach, but don't forget to check out the schedule of the Mobile BayBears!

Find out more:
Mobile BayBears
Mobile, AL 36606
Phone: 251-479-2327

TAMPA BAY RAYS
Minor league baseball has become a big hit in the Southeast with the new teams building stadiums or adding to existing ones to make the fan experience unique as they cross the region traveling to watch the game. The Montgomery Biscuits, minor league affiliate of the Tampa Bay Rays, have made the dream come true by bringing baseball to the capital city in 2004. So, for a season of stealing bases and strikeout pitches at the Riverwalk Stadium, make plans now!

Find out more:
Montgomery Biscuits Baseball
Montgomery, AL
Phone: 334-323-2255
Website: biscuitsbaseball.com

SAN FRANCISCO GIANTS

You won't find the Golden Gate Bridge, but you will discover a connection to the west coast. The 2004 season of minor league ball began a new period for the fans that travel to see the future pros of the big leagues compete in northeast Georgia. Augusta baseball dates back before the turn of the 20th century and has seen several organizations that represented various major league teams. Presently, the San Francisco Giants' minor league team plays at Augusta's Lake Olmstead Stadium.

Find out more:
Lake Olmstead Stadium
78 Milledge Road
Augusta, GA 30904
Phone: 706-736-7889
Website: GreenJackets.net

ROME BRAVES
The "City of Seven Hills" hosts a favorite of northwest Georgia fans. With some of the best deals and one of the most fun choices of entertainment, the Rome Braves calls Floyd County home. This team moved from Macon and has been playing in Rome since 2003. Have one of the world famous hot dogs at the Three Rivers Club, the

61

stadium restaurant. Have fun watching the minor league team play ball at State Mutual Stadium. Buy a ticket for one of the bleacher seats, or bring a lawn chair and sit in the grass area. If you think the regular seats are a great price, then wait and see what the cost is for saving a spot on the lawn. Don't forget to check out the gift shop while you are there!

Find out more:
Rome Braves
Rome, GA
Phone: 706-378-5100
Website: Romebraves.com

MORE BRAVES

Some may consider themselves fair weather fans, but there are those who cannot get enough of Atlanta Braves baseball; and there is more than one minor league team! Each one is a step closer to playing in the major leagues. For those proud of the Atlanta Braves, attend a game and see where the players of tomorrow are discovered. The Gwinnett Braves invite fans traveling through town, or locals, to come for one of the best deals money can buy.

Find out more:
Gwinnett Braves
Phone: 678-277-0300
Website: GwinnettBraves.com

COLORADO ROCKIES

A great combination for sport fans that travel to the Biltmore Estate would be to include a game to watch the Asheville Tourists play minor league ball. McCormick Field opened in 1924 and has many affiliations with many major leagues, but today the Colorado Rockies' minor league team, the Asheville Tourists, grace the field as fans flock to the stadium. For those who remember the movie, "Bull Durham" with Kevin Costner, the Tourists had a small role in the film.

Find out more:
Asheville Tourists
Asheville, NC
Phone: 826-258-0428

HOW ABOUT THOSE YANKEES?

Charleston has been a baseball town since 1885. More than two million over the decades have visited the stadium to watch their minor league team play. Other affiliates have been a part of the Charleston history. However, 1995 began an affiliation with the New York Yankees. Why travel to New York when you can get a taste in the Southeast?

Find out more:
Charleston RiverDogs
Charleston, SC
Phone: 843-723-7241
Website: riverdogs.com

THE BOSTON RED SOX

For those who remember the movie, "Field of Dreams," the name Shoeless Joe Jackson may come to mind. He was a native of Greenville and would have been a Hall of Famer because of his role in baseball during the early 19th century. However, he was accused of being involved in fixing the World Series of 1919. While evidence may prove his innocence, some wanted the Greenville team to be awarded the name to be given in his honor as a historic figure. Some say that Babe Ruth adopted his batting style after Shoeless Joe Jackson. In 2004, the Drive became an affiliate of the Boston Red Sox. Make plans to attend a Fluor Field at the West End game where more than 350,000 have flocked to see in a regular season. The park was built similar to Fenway Park, the home of the Boston Red Sox.

Find out more:
Fluor Field at the West End
Greenville Drive
Greenville, SC
Phone: 864-240-4500
Website: GreenvilleDrive.com

FLORIDA MARLINS

Marlin fans can take a trip to Miami or visit a closer destination to the Florida coast and watch a game on the home field of the Jacksonville Suns. Since 1904, professional baseball in Jacksonville has had Hall of Famers like Phil Niekro, Hank Aaron, Tom Seaver, Nolan Ryan, Hoyt Wilhelm, and many others who have since retired. Several of today's major league players have run the bases in the state's largest city of Duvall County. Several major league affiliations have had connections to Jacksonville as the training camp for their minor league teams. In 2003, a new stadium was built and by the fourth season the Jacksonville Suns had welcomed their 1,000,000th fan. In 2009, the Jacksonville Suns had become an affiliate of the Florida Marlins. It looks like it may be an exciting season in the coming years at this historic field.

Find out more:
Jacksonville Suns
Jacksonville, FL
Phone: 904-358-2846
Website: Jaxsuns.com

MINNESOTA TWINS
Chattanooga built a new stadium in 2000. The year 2009 started an affiliation with the Los Angeles Dodgers as the parent club for the Lookouts. The Chattanooga Lookouts celebrate their 130th season during 2015. Several major leaguers have run the bases as a Lookout, such as Burleigh Grimes, Harmon Killebrew, Alvin Davis, Pete Rose Jr., and many others. The Chattanooga Lookouts became an affiliate of the Minnesota Twins in 2015.

Find out more:
Chattanooga Lookouts
Chattanooga, TN
Phone: 423-267-2208
Website: lookouts.com

MORE MINNESOTA TWINS

With the backdrop of the Appalachian Mountains on the banks of the scenic Watauga River, this small town has been home to the Elizabethton Twins since 1974. The year 2010 marked the 36th anniversary of the Minnesota Twins' affiliations with this club. If you enjoy the beauty of the Appalachian region, plan a few days in northeast Tennessee. Make a side trip to watch a team play that has not had a losing streak since 1989.

Find out more:
Elizabethton Twins
Elizabethton, TN
Phone: 423-547-6441
Website: Elizabethtontwins.com

CHICAGO CUBS
Come to the Smoky Mountain National Park. Make a visit to Smoky Mountain Visitor Center in Kodak, Tennessee, where you can find all you need to know about the attractions in the National Park. At this time, the Chicago Cubs are the parent affiliation of the minor league team of the Tennessee Smokies. The team has had a variety of changes since the organization of the baseball club in 1909. For a taste of Chicago baseball, buy a ticket at the visitor center.

Find out more:
Tennessee Smokies
Kodak, TN
Phone: 865-286-2300
Website: smokiesbaseball.com

DINNER AND A SHOW

Featuring community theater productions, plays, orchestras, concerts, and more favorites across the South

The backdrop of downtown Chatsworth, Georgia at the Welcome Center on Route 411 just south of the Tennessee state line. Literally a gateway to the Georgia Smokies.

DINNER AND A SHOW

Featured community theater productions, plays, orchestra, concerts, and more favorites across the South

Most will never engrave their star next to John Wayne, Lucille Ball, Betty Grable, Charlie Chaplin, or W.C. Fields, much less anyone on the stretch of sidewalk of downtown Hollywood. But most will get their beginnings in the small community theater. Who knows the talent yet to be discovered? These local productions are performed by those who we know and are very entertaining. While regional and national talent may bring their show to the small community stage, there is still something to be said about local folks who shared part of themselves to make us laugh, cry, or simply to entertain us.

Some of the stages celebrate a historical benchmark that has been around for decades and are still a strong presence in the region. Others have had national recognition, and have received awards for their excellent achievements. Still, one may find a simple stage with down-home folks who simply have a story to tell, and they do a great job! We have included a wide range of local productions which offer a variety of dinner shows, orchestras, plays, and comedies. The possibilities are endless! Everyone of any age can enjoy community theater. Its birth dates back for centuries before the big screen was ever invented. One will find some opportunities in our backyard, while some may have to travel a distance around the southwestern Appalachian foothills across state lines. If that is the case, most will find these side trips worth the consideration to add to your vacation or quick getaway.

So, from gospel to bluegrass, musicals to performances, check out the region for a taste of local celebrities for an evening to remember!

1902 STOCK EXCHANGE

Hidden off the beaten path is the downtown district of Adairsville in Bartow County in northwest Georgia. It is a must-stop for travelers who have a few moments to dine at Maggie Mae's Cafe' and Tea Room, or attend one of the seasonal dinner theaters at the Opera House. This historic building was remodeled in 1994 and has been an attraction for locals and tourists since it opened its doors. They are convenient to the expressway and there are an abundance of area attractions that Bartow County has to offer.

Find out more:
The 1902 Stock Exchange
Adairsville, GA
Phone: 770-773-1902

THE TOWNSEND CENTER

On the campus of the University of West Georgia is a venue well known to the area for its performing arts programs at the Center. Keeping up with the events throughout the year, you will be amazed at the variety of talent that is on the books for the coming seasons. Buy your tickets in advance for your favorite artist, or try something new. Watch one of the on-campus performances for an enjoyable evening.

Find out more:
The Townsend Center
Carrollton, GA
Phone: 678-839-4722
Website: TownsendCenter.org

HOLLY THEATER

The historic district of Dahlonega has its own award winning performances. The Mountain Music and Medicine Show is a popular show by locals. It takes a look at the early mid-19th century. The show looks at local history, culture, and humor. The tickets are reasonable for every seat in the house. Check the schedule and plan to spend some time in the town before the show.

Find out more:
Holly Theater
Dahlonega, GA
Phone: 706-864-3759
Website: hollytheater.com

MABLE HOUSE AMPHITHEATER

The Mable House has been a historic site for decades, since it was used during the Civil War by the federal troops. It was one of the few structures that was not burned in the path of the Union Army. Today, it has an amphitheater that seats 2,400 guests for concerts ranging from local talent to big-name artists, with performances covering a wide variety of interests.

Find out more:
Mable House Amphitheater
Mableton, GA
Phone: 770-819-7765
Website: mablehouse.org

SWAMP GRAVY

Now, here is a community theater that has been in the news, major publications, and they even have a volunteer team that travels out of town to give folks in other communities a taste of what life is like in south Georgia. Somehow folks who attend go away feeling like they can relate to the stories that are told. Folks travel to and from the coast to watch one of the live performances professionally written, choreographed, and produced, then it's retold by the community themselves.

Find out more:
Swamp Gravy
Colquitt, GA
Phone: 229-758-5450

ROME SYMPHONY ORCHESTRA
The South's oldest symphony calls Floyd County, Georgia home. Throughout the year, they perform around the area. They have shared their music since 1921. In almost another decade they will celebrate their 100th birthday. Check out their calendar of seasonal programs.

Find out more:
Rome Symphony Orchestra
Rome, GA
Phone: 706-291-7967
Website: romesymphony.org

PASSION PLAY IN THE SMOKIES

More than a play! Experience the story of the Lord Jesus when He walked the streets of Jerusalem. Attend one of the many events during the year. Let the Bible come to life! See live re-enactments. Watch a performance of the Passion Play that shows Christ's last days before the crucifixion and after the resurrection. On your next visit to the Smokies, check out the calendar so you can attend a performance.

Find out more:
Passion Play in the Smokies
Townsend, TN
Phone: 865-448-3505

BLUE RIDGE COMMUNITY THEATER

One of the gems of north Georgia is the Blue Ridge Scenic Railway located in Blue Ridge, Georgia. It takes you down the tracks along the Toccoa River for about 18 miles to the town of McCaysville. There are more shops and things to see. One more thing you may want to consider is the performing arts schedule at the Blue Ridge Community Theater, where you can see the performances of local talent.

Find out more:
Blue Ridge Community Theater
Blue Ridge, GA
Phone: 706-632-9223
Website: BlueRidgeCommunityTheater.com

GADSDEN CONVENTION HALL AND HISTORIC MORT GLOSSER AMPHITHEATER

Community theater is a growing trend. Learn about the opportunities for concerts, dramas, and other performances at the amphitheater in Etowah County, Alabama. Among other local activities in the area are Noccalula Falls Park and Tigers for Tomorrow.

Find out more:
Historic Mort Glosser Amphitheater
Gadsden, AL
Phone: 256-549-4669
Website: gadsden-etowahtourismboard.com

WETUMPKA DEPOT PLAYERS

Celebrating thirty years of performances, it all started with an idea to raise money to save the town's historic district. They used their local talent to put on a community theater that would continue for decades. In 1999, they were able to purchase an old grocery store and continue to make people laugh and cry to a packed out audience!

Find out more:
Wetumpka Depot Players
Wetumpka, AL
Phone: 334-868-1440
Website: wetumpkadepot.com

LIVE BIBLICAL PRODUCTIONS

This production company has become an attraction to folks through South Carolina as many watch the Bible come alive. The calendar is filled with professional shows telling scenes given in the Old Testament and New Testament. See the miracles of Jesus. Experience the first Christmas. Watch the Easter story unfold. Plan to come to one of the dinner shows for the journey of a lifetime during one of these quality productions.

Find out more:
NarroWay Productions
Fort Mill, SC
Phone: 803-802-2300
Website: Narroway.net

THE DALLAS THEATER

Paulding County, Georgia, is a gateway to the Appalachian Mountains. Nestled in the northwest region of the state, it is filled with outdoor adventure, Civil War history, driving tours, and more! The Dallas Theater is becoming a major venue in the county. Watch out! The Paulding Players are making their own history as they begin a season entertaining their audiences. Over the next decade, only time will reveal the talent that will unfold on this very stage. Concerts, shows, and other programs make this an exciting place for those who live in the local area or guests who will come through town.

Find out more:
The Dallas Theater
Dallas, GA
Phone: 770-445-5180
Website: dallastheater-civiccenter.com

THE WHOLE BACKSTAGE

This community theater has been the talk of the town since 1968 when they started from humble beginnings. Today, they are still performing in the beautiful region of Guntersville, Alabama. The community theater has been written about in Southern Living magazine. Hopefully, it will continue as a family tradition for years to come. There are a lot of reasons to come to Guntersville, Alabama. While you are here, consider scheduling one of their performances. One of the performances that you won't want to miss is the live Christmas production of "A Christmas Story," with Ralphie as he tells his story of growing up in the 1940s.

Find out more:
Whole Backstage
Guntersville, AL 35976
Phone: 256-582-7469
Website: wholebackstage.com

THE GRAND THEATER

Since 1929, this community theater has brought various talent into town and has brought concerts and community to the stage. You will want to check out the seasonal scheduling to get an idea of the variety of shows that are being performed. Bartow County, Georgia, is filled with plenty of attractions and great restaurants. Top it off with performance at The Grand Theatre.

Find out more:
The Grand Theatre
Cartersville, GA
Phone: 770-386-7343
Website: thegrandtheatre.org

MIRACLE WORKER

Imagine having an opportunity to stand in front of the President and other government officials to give a speech in Washington, DC. Imagine having eyes that could not see the faces to whom you were speaking, or voicing sounds that were clear to those around you without ever hearing a sound coming from your own lips. Wonder what it would be like to only be able to have all responses interpreted to you by the few who could communicate to a person who is both deaf and blind?

Helen Keller is known around the world and her story begins in a small rural town in the Appalachian foothills of north Alabama. As an educator, she opened doors to help many, when most would have given them the title of "holiness." Born in 1880, she would develop a rare disease that would leave her deaf and blind for the rest of her life. Yet, when someone took the time to communicate with her world, she became a beacon of hope for future generations.

Find out more:
Tuscumbia, AL
Phone: 256-383-4066
Website: helenkellerbirthplace.org

LIBERTY DRAMA

A really neat place is the Bicentennial Capitol Mall State Park. Each year it celebrates with the Tennessee Historical Festival. There is a performance at the amphitheater re-enacting the events as they unfold of the founding of the state of Tennessee. Also, check out the other events at the amphitheater in Music City USA.

Find out more:
Bicentennial Capitol Mall State Park
Nashville, TN
Phone: 615-741-5280
Website: Liberty-Drama.com

WILDERNESS THEATER
The world's largest outdoor theater is in the northwest corner of Georgia. The theater features mostly family films. Drive up, watch, and listen from the convenience of your own vehicle. Food is available at the theater in case you get hungry. There are a lot of things to do during the day in this region of the state. With proper planning, you can have

a blast all day long! Close to Chattanooga and north Georgia attractions.

Find out more:
Wilderness Outdoor Theater
Trenton, GA
Phone: 706-657-8411
Website: wildernesstheater.com

MILL TOWN MUSIC HALL

One of northwest Georgia's largest attractions of its type, they offer to the local community some of the leading concerts and entertainment that is wholesome for the whole family. They are becoming increasingly well known, and have put Bremen on the map for folks who travel across the region. Check out their calendar for performances for families, church groups, and a variety of groups that will enjoy.
More info:
Mill Town Music Hall
Bremen, GA
Phone: 770-537-6455
Website: milltownmusichall.com

QUAINT SHOPS & SOUTHERN SECRETS

Featured small towns, Christmas shops, specialty stores, and more favorites across the South

Can you guess which historic town this is? Discover small town America in the Appalachian Foothills!

QUAINT SHOPS SOUTHERN SECRETS
Featured small towns, Christmas shops, specialty stores

While the book lists small rural towns, specific stores were not listed. We have listed websites and contact information to aid you in your shopping excursion. While some of the areas may have a variety of choices to keep you browsing for hours, other communities may have only a few and they still make great stops when you are traveling through the area. In most of these areas, there are a number of local attractions and great restaurants to make your journey to the region worth the drive. So, if it's a girls' night out, a church ladies retreat, or a family outing, take a trip and find the one little treasure to help you remember the time spent with your family and friends.

DALLAS AND HIRAM

Paulding County was named after John Paulding, who became a war hero when he helped arrest a man who was plotting with Benedict Arnold to betray the American government at the time of the American Revolution. During the Civil War, a significant surprise took place when the Union Army could burst through the enemy lines and advance toward Atlanta sooner. The Confederates waited until Sherman's men made their move and fought through the night defeating the Union Army three to one. In this area, one of the many things to do is spend your time browsing some of the unique shops. Dallas and Hiram have a variety of shops in and around the historic districts. There are arts, crafts, and specialty gift shops. You will like the variety of choices while browsing the small town district. Some of the best cooking in the area can be found in the local restaurants, although some local proprietors may be closed on Mondays.

Find out more:
Paulding County, GA
Phone: 770-445-6016
Website: pauldingchamber.org

VILLA RICA AND CARROLLTON, GEORGIA
Carroll County was named after one of the signers of the Declaration of Independence who lived in the territory. The city of Villa Rica was established in 1826 and became one of the country's first Gold Rush towns. When miners found gold in Villa Rica in the 1820's, some say the discovery was older than the one found in Dahlonega, Georgia. The train stopped years ago, letting off passengers. Now, the historic downtown is lined with a variety of great tasting restaurants, a few antique and gift shops that make this a good stop along the way! Take some time to visit the county seat of Carrollton for more restaurants and treasures to find.

Find out more:
Website: Villaricatourism.com
Website: Visitcarrollton.com

CARTERSVILLE AND ADAIRSVILLE, GEORGIA

Bartow County's historic heritage ranges from famous gangsters to public figures. Most locals do not realize the treasures that can be found here, with all the museums and historic sites, to the land of the cowboys and Indians, adventure awaits! For those wanting to spend some time on a leisurely day, the inspirational stories of people such as Evangelist Sam Jones and Lottie Moon are worth the distance. While you are creating an itinerary, don't forget to browse the variety of shops nearby. The shops around the downtown districts of Cartersville and Adairsville are a must stop in northwest Georgia. There are a variety of gift shops, apparel shops, antique shops, crafts and collectibles, auctions, home decor shops, outlets, and sporting goods/outfitters. Folks come from every direction to spend the day with a variety of things to do.

Find out more:
Cartersville, GA
Phone: 770-387-1357 or 800-733-2280
Website: VisitCartersvilleGa.org

DAHLONEGA, GEORGIA

The first major gold rush was made in 1828. The federal government had planned at the turn of the century to move the Native Americans west. A decade after the discovery of gold, the Native Americans would be forced from their settlements across the Southeast. As settlers came, they pioneered the regions across the state. The town of Dahlonega has grown into a popular destination as tourists travel across north Georgia. For a taste of local flavor, there are a number of restaurants. Are you looking for a unique gift? Visit an old general store, a glass blowing shop, gift shops, art galleries, outfitters, and a variety of other specialty shops that will keep you browsing!

Find out more:
Dahlonega-Lumpkin County Visitors Center
Dahlonega, GA
Phone: 706-864-3711
Website: dahlonega.org

HELEN, GEORGIA

Only Savannah and Atlanta host more guests than those who come to Helen as tourists. They come from all over the nation and would see this historic town in the southwestern region of the Appalachian foothills. It is in our own back yard and is very close to visit. Of course, during Oktoberfest, traffic is bumper-to-bumper, but off season it is much easier to come for a visit! The downtown district looks like a Bavarian alpine town in Germany. It has a variety of specialty shops, gift shops, apparel, home decor, and much more. This is a favorite destination for a quick getaway that folks all over Georgia and the surrounding area visit throughout the year.

Find out more:
Helen, GA
Phone: 706-878-2181
Website: helenga.org

BLUE RIDGE, GEORGIA

The Cohutta Mountains meander through north Georgia and become the Smoky Mountains in Tennessee. Who said you had to travel far to enjoy a taste of the Smoky

Mountain region? The town of Blue Ridge is a must stop for a quick getaway. Historic Blue Ridge and McCaysville are filled with unique shops and restaurants. Blue Ridge has been called the "Antique Capital of Georgia." These districts are a great place to find local crafts, beautiful art, pottery, homemade clothing, and more. Spend an hour or several hours browsing. Don't forget to make a visit to the local orchard for some of the best apples, only found in north Georgia!

Find out more:
Blue Ridge, GA
Phone: 706-632-5680 or 800-899-6867
Website: blueridgemountains.com

DALTON, GEORGIA

When folks say Dalton, people first think of this town being known as the "Carpet Capital of the World." In the early 1900s bedspreads were made for income from one of the local merchants. Bedspreads were hung along the Dixie Highway from north Georgia to the south. The construction of Highway 41 made the bedspreads more visible to tourists as they travelled to Florida on vacation. With the most popular bedspread sold that had a peacock design on the front, the region became known as 'Peacock Alley." From this industry, the carpet business grew. Dalton produced 80% of the world's carpet, but this is not all it produced. The town is filled with antique shops, outlet shops, malls, specialty shops and more. There are a variety of shops along the historic downtown district as well. You definitely cannot browse them all in one day!

Find out more:
Phone: 706-270-9960
Website: visitdaltonga.org

CALHOUN, GEORGIA

A visit to the settlement of New Echota is worth the trip. It is the last capitol of the Cherokee nation. One will see a village made by the Cherokee with farms, a school, newspaper, church, and three branches of government. The newspaper is still running after almost 200 years out west. Calhoun has several shops in the historic downtown district filled with antiques and more. Don't forget to check out the Prime Outlet store with a host of name brand merchandise. There are also plenty of great restaurants for those who want their favorite franchise to local flavor, only found in Calhoun.

Find out more:
Gordon County, GA
Phone: 706-625-3200
Website: exploregordoncounty.org

CHICKAMAUGA, GEORGIA

When you are traveling to the Chattanooga area, don't forget a side trip to the small historic district of Chickamauga, Georgia. There are a few shops to browse for that unique keepsake that may add to your leisurely journey on the way home. Walk through a variety of antique shops. Take a moment to check out the old general store.

Find out more:
Website: cityofchickamauga.org

ACWORTH, KENNESAW AND MARIETTA, GEORGIA

Along Cobb County's stretch of the Dixie Highway, discover a southern flavor that takes you back to a different era where the towns are dotted with historic homes and old-fashioned main streets lined with unique shops, local cafes, antiques, galleries, and treasures. This is the only fraction of the Dixie Highway that was built in the 1920s with plans to be more than 5,700 miles long. It would've stretched from Canada in the north and southward, deep into the state of Florida. So, you can experience part of the historic drive. When you are passing through the area, come for a visit.

Find out more:
Website: TravelCobb.org

LOOKOUT MOUNTAIN

At the south end of the Lookout Mountain Parkway as it crosses over the Alabama border, one will find a wide variety of treasures around the Dekalb County area. From hand-made arts and crafts, one of Alabama's largest locally owned furniture stores, antiques, galleries, specialty shops, a unique blown glass studio, and more. Check out the opportunities that may keep you busy for a long time!

Find out more:
Phone: 888-805-4740
Website: tourdekalb.com

ROME AND CAVE SPRING, GEORGIA
Rome is a beautiful place with a number of hills and valleys rolling through the landscapes among three rivers that have been given Indian names. In Floyd County, Berry College has become an icon of sorts. It is known as the world's largest college campus. Cave Spring is a city in Floyd County, as well. The town has a few surprises of its own. The water from the creek has been used to sell to local vendors as drinking water. A small cave is located in the local park and can be toured for a small fee. One of the largest outdoor public pools in the state is built in the shape of Georgia. You will want to check out the opportunities in the historic districts of Rome and Cave Spring. The Floyd County area offers a variety of surprises waiting to be discovered! Find a unique gift or an old antique. There is an abundance of things to do, including popular cafes and franchised restaurants to make your visit worth the trip.

Find out more:
Rome and Cave Spring
Phone: 706-295-5576 or 800-444-1834
Website: RomeGeorgia.org

GADSDEN AND ATTALLA, ALABAMA

Gadsden was a stagecoach stop between Huntsville and Rome after it was established in 1825 as the town of

Double Springs. The original home that was built in the mid 1820s still stands as the oldest structure in the town. The Coosa River would be used to pilot ferry boats to the area for transportation in the later 1800s. Attalla was the site of a Creek Indian village and important during the Indian War, referred to as the Red-Stick War between 1813 and 1814. Unless you have taken some time to meander to the southern end of the Lookout Mountain Parkway, you don't know what you have been missing! The historic town district of Gadsden has been remodeled and there are some antique and specialty shops. Attalla has three blocks of antique and specialty shops in the historic district.

Find out more:
Downtown Gadsden and Attalla
Phone: 256-549-0351
Website: greatergadsden.com

FOOD EXCURSIONS

Featured tea rooms, coffee shops, cafes, breakfasts, burgers, barbecue, steak, seafood, fine dining, and more southern favorites.

Dine on the river. Enjoy an outside meal located on a scenic brow. While sitting in an old historic depot, listen as the trains pass through. There is a taste for everyone in the Appalachian foothills.

APPALACHIAN FOOD EXCURSIONS
Featured Tea Rooms, Coffee Shops, Cafes, Breakfast,
Burgers, BBQ, Steak, Seafood, Fine Dining, and more
Southern Favorites.

Where can you find local favorites when traveling around
the southwestern region of the Appalachian foothills? Ask
around and locals will tell you! Here are some of those
local gems off the beaten path. Some are small tea shops
and cafes. Others are known for their barbecue, steaks,
and seafood. Still, some offer the unique fine dining
experience to those special occasions. The days they are
open may vary, as well as the hours. A few may be open
daily, serving three meals a day. Others may serve only
two and open a few days during the week. Depending on
the location is a quaint, rural town or a larger city dining
experience. So, break away from traditional tastes you find
in major chains and try local flavor, voted number one by
those who often travel through the area. Church groups,
school groups, families, and business travelers can find
that special dining experience that may keep you coming
back. When you plan your next visit, consider in your
itinerary time to visit some of the local history landmarks,
nature attractions, and other venues that make it a
different place from all the rest.

THURSTON'S CAFE
A great place in Calhoun for lunch! Try their soups, salads,
sandwiches, and desserts. Located in the historic district of
Calhoun, convenient to Interstate 75 and along the Dixie
Highway off Route 41. There are some things to do in the
area from shopping to historical landmarks.

Find out more:
Thurston's Cafe
Calhoun, GA
Phone: 706-602-4401

MAGGIE MAE'S TEA ROOM

One would never dream what they could find unless they passed this way! This quaint, historic district has made local news all over north Georgia. The remodeling of the building was an undertaking that has paid off and become a staple to the community. Today, it is a gift shop, tea room, and opera house where they have seasonal programs. You will want to try one of their lunch menu items when coming through the area. It is convenient to the expressway and many local attractions.

Find out more:
Maggie Mae's
1902 Stock Exchange
Adairsville, GA
Phone: 770-773-1902

OAKWOOD CAFE

The restaurant has been around for almost 100 years. It has become a landmark in Dalton, Georgia, that serves three meals per day. They serve a wide variety of breakfast items made fresh to order. In fact, they say if you don't feel like family, they want to know! They have a menu serving barbecue, baby-back ribs, chicken, country vegetables, sandwiches, desserts, and more. They must have done things right to have been a favorite for so many decades.

Find out more:
Oakwood Cafe
(located downtown)
Dalton, GA
Phone: 706-529-9663
Website: oakwoodcafe.net

GABRIEL'S DESSERTS

Are you familiar with Paula Deen? Her cousin, Johnnie Gabriel, has a taste you need to try! Good cooking is a family trait. For years, Johnnie Gabriel has been cooking and sharing her fabulous food. The Gabriels began baking at night using family recipes to support their family's income. For more than a decade, the restaurant has hired professional chefs to make from scratch homemade cakes, cookies, pies, and other delicious desserts. Today, Gabriel's Desserts has a delicious menu for breakfast, lunch, and dinner six days a week. They are conveniently located not too far from the historic Marietta Square in Cobb County, Georgia.

Find out more:
Gabriel's Desserts
Marietta, GA
Phone: 770-427-9007
Website: gabrielsdesserts.com

BAR-L BAR-B-QUE

Not too far from Rockmart's downtown area on Elm Street sits one of the best deals and great tastes in the area. There is a good selection from the menu for lunch and dinner. They have a good number of basket selections, and their customer service is friendly! The food comes out hot, fresh, and within a reasonable amount of time. One of the local attractions is the Silver Comet Trail that runs through the park in town. There are a number of historic sites and unique shops that are close.

Find out more:
Bar-L Bar-B-Que
Rockmart, GA
Phone: 770-684-2656

CHEESEBURGER BOBBY'S

Not often do folks get to dine at the original location where it all began. But, since 2007, Cheeseburger Bobby's has been growing to become "the best burger in town." They have definitely won the hearts of Hiram, Georgia. It all started with their grand opening, when they offered free food for a year. People brought cots, sleeping bags, and their vehicles to be the first to wait in line. People have been standing in line for lunch and dinner ever since. Today, they are expanding to several locations, but there is something really cool about dining where the first burger was served to the first customer! It truly is the small-town burger place, offering fresh food and friendly customer service in a relaxing atmosphere. It's a great place for families, church groups, school groups, and business groups. They are conveniently located near sites, driving tours, bike trails, and outdoor adventure.

Find out more:
Cheeseburger Bobby's
Hiram, GA
Phone: 678-567-2037
Website: cheeseburgerbobbys.com

THE STEAKHOUSE

Yes, that's what it's called! Locals and guests from the area know all about it. It is located off Highway 278 in a farming community in the town of Rockmart. Many who discover it often return for some of the best steaks in and around the county. There are some nearby historic attractions. The Silver Comet Trail meanders nearby the area. There are definitely a lot of local things to do within an hour's drive of Polk County.

Find out more:
The Steakhouse
Rockmart, GA 30153
Phone: 770-684-0401

BACKWOODS STEAK HOUSE

If you ask the folks around Haralson County about the best restaurants in the area, they would include this restaurant in the list! They are not on main streets and unless you hear of it through word of mouth, you may not know it's there! Driving on the back roads in the rural town of

Tallapoosa, Georgia, you will discover what makes this a repeat of locals around the region.

Find out more:
Backwoods Steak House
Tallapoosa, GA 30176-2240
Phone: 770-574-7050

DUB'S HIGH ON THE HOG

Some of the best food in the area is located at Dub's near downtown Calhoun, Georgia. Try their prime rib, barbecue chicken, and many other menu choices that offer a delicious variety for every taste. The customer service is friendly and usually fast! You definitely will want to come with a hearty appetite. It's definitely a winner to the locals in the area!

Find out more:
Dub's High on the Hog
Calhoun, GA
Phone: 706-602-5150

BOWMAN'S RESTAURANT

You may pass the Resaca exit on Interstate 75 and head for one of those same tastes that are everywhere, or you can venture off and find a restaurant that cooks home-grown vegetables from its own farm. That's what you will find when you dine at Bowman's. They have a saying, "Everything is as good as my mother made it."

Find out more:
Bowman's
Resaca, GA
Phone: 706-624-3255
Website: bowmansrestaurantandcatering.com

MARIETTA DINER

The diner has become a staple in the northwest Atlanta area for several years. A touch of New York, Greek, and southern flavor makes this twenty-four hour operation a favorite place to eat. So, if it's time for breakfast, lunch, or dinner, there is something for every taste. You may have seen them on the Food Network program "Diners, Drive-Ins, and Dives."

Find out more:
Marietta Diner
Marietta, GA 30060
Phone: 770-423-9390
Website: mariettadiner.net

APPALACHIAN GRILL

Under the bridge in downtown Cartersville is one of the area's favorite grills. With steak, seafood, sandwiches, and a variety of other choices, one will find the food delicious and customer service first class. They have a variety of delicious appetizers, desserts, and more. They are open for lunch and dinner Monday through Friday.

Find out more:
Appalachian Grill
Cartersville, GA
Phone: 770-607-5357

DALTON DEPOT

Relive history at the 1852 Dalton Depot. They have been
serving locals and those traveling through northwest
Georgia since 1990. There are a variety of menu choices
for lunch or dinner. Try one of the appetizers from Buffalo
wings, tenderloin tips, gourmet pizzas, and more. They
also serve a variety of soups, salads, sandwiches, and
burgers in addition to steaks, seafood, and other entree
choices.

Find out more:
Dalton Depot
Dalton, GA
Phone: 706-226-3160
Website: thedaltondepot.net

TOP O' THE RIVER

One of the Southeast's largest catfish and seafood
restaurants opened their first location in Anniston,
Alabama. Now they have locations across north Alabama.
Folks travel from all over to eat some of the best seafood
in the Appalachian foothills. Each customer receives a
hearty portion made fresh daily. They have a variety of
appetizers, catfish, seafood, chicken, steak, and desserts.

Find out more:
Top O' the River
Anniston, AL
Phone: 256-238-0097
Website: topoftheriverrestaurant.com

CHATTANOOGA CHOO CHOO

The town of Chattanooga plays host to some of America's
most well known tourist attractions. Among them is the
Chattanooga Choo Choo. The terminal station was spared
from destruction in the early 1970's. Today, it is a historical
landmark offering services only the wealthier would have
had access to during the heyday of the Chattanooga Choo
Choo. It is definitely a place for special occasions and
events since its restoration. Check out the fine dining and
first-class lodging opportunities.

Find out more:
Chattanooga Choo Choo
Chattanooga, TN
800-Track-29
Website: ChooChoo.com

HENRY'S LOUISIANA GRILL

Along the Dixie Highway, there are a variety of things to do
for a leisurely day. However, folks are talking about the
taste of Louisiana in the heart of Acworth! They come from
all over to dine at Henry's. Choose from a selection of
fresh homemade entrees and desserts. You will want to
ask about hosting special events. There is a variety of

menu choices made especially by the chef for your group. The food is as first class as the customer service!

Find out more:
Henry's Louisiana Grill
Acworth, GA
Phone: 770-966-1515
Website: chefhenrys.com

UDDER DELIGHTS
Some of the best southern cooking you have ever put in your mouth. They have a good variety for every taste bud that enters the door. The portions have always been a good size. The desserts are delicious. Before you leave, save some room for one of their famous banana splits, floats, sundaes, and more. Their ice cream shop is second to none. This gem is located on Highway 113 between Rockmart and Cartersville. If you are making a side trip to browse the shops or museums around the historic districts of these communities, this is convenient from either direction.

More info:
2351 Highway 113
Cartersville, GA 30178
Phone: 770-387-9188

GALLERY ROW

On the square in the downtown district of Carrollton, Georgia. With all of the attractions in Carrollton, Gallery Row is worth the stop. It's a great place to grab a bite for breakfast and lunch. They offer a variety of dessert items. Some of their main specialties are the large selection of coffees and teas. Learn something new about the different blends, and some of their own favorites.

More info:
Gallery Row
Historic Downtown
Carrollton, GA
Phone: 770-832-1455
Website: galleryrowcoffee.com

COTTAGE TREASURES

This is a must stop for those who meander around the top of Northwest Georgia. They serve delicious lunches during the week. They have a good menu your taste buds will be in for a treat. They serve a variety of soups, salads and a variety of entrees. Folks enjoy their selection of teas. They also have a gift shop where one can find a unique keepsake from a variety of tea cups, tea pots, to a variety of related pieces. Also, they have home decor items, and ideas for special occasions. Plan to visit one of their open houses throughout the year for Spring, Mother's Day, Fall, and Christmas.

For more info:

Cottage Treasures
Ringgold, GA
Phone: 706-935-2548
Website: CottageTreasures.com

The Fish Market

Ask around town if you are craving seafood. Many of the locals will probably say you have to try the Fish Market. They have been around for several years as a favorite for those driving into town, or who live in the area. Good places to eat are worth driving the distance.

For more info:

The Fish Market
1504 Rainbow Drive
Gadsden, Alabama
Phone: 256-547-4141
Website: fishmarketgadsden.com

Stay In The Foothills

Meander along one of the many historic routes in the Appalachian foothills

Don't forget your camera to capture memories!

STAY AND PLAY GETAWAYS

Featured RV Rentals, Floating Condos, Historic Inns, On the Lake, Mountain Views, Cabins, Resorts, and more Southern Favorites

From romantic getaways to simple family outings, discover bed and breakfasts, resorts, camping, mountain bike getaways, guest ranches, and more. Around the Southwestern region of the Appalachian foothills, one will find nestled along country roads treasures worth discovering. Word of mouth is often how folks learn of where to find them, or it simply happens when folks stumble across the path and wish they had scheduled their lodging there. Here are a few such places with a wide variety of services and amenities for every occasion. They are not in any given order. Some will have first class lodging, catering to those who are desiring to celebrate the special romantic getaway or anniversary. Others will be looking for simple camping or a unique lodging experience. Still, there is a maze of adventure in the list of packages, pleasing a variety of interests.

THE RAGSDALE INN

Step back in time to the early 1900s, forty years after the Civil War. This beautiful Victorian home is nestled in the foothills near the historic district of downtown Dallas, Georgia. The home is convenient to unique shops, great cafes with local flavor, historic tours, and many nearby attractions. Enjoy relaxing on the huge, rocking-chair front porch, or perhaps take a ride along Georgia's well known, 90-mile Silver Comet Trail.

Find out more:
The Ragsdale Inn
Dallas, GA
Phone: 770-443-3440
Website: theragsdaleinn.com

CEDAR CREEK PARK

For family fun on a budget, try Cedar Creek Park. Reserve a campsite, RV site, or lodging. Rent a kayak, canoe, or tube for floating down Big Cedar Creek. Try the golf range, or other activities at the park. They are close to many attractions. Go to a Rome Braves minor league baseball game. Browse some of the local shops. Dine at one of the local cafes. Among the outdoor activities in the area, there is a range of such things as scenic drives, hiking trails, state parks, horseback riding, and the list seems endless!

Find out more:
Cedar Creek RV & Driving Range
Cave Spring, GA 30124
Phone: 706-777-3030
Website: bigcedarcreek.com

MOUNTAIN BIKE GETAWAY

In the Chattahoochee National Forest and the Cohutta Wilderness are breathtaking views along the trails in one of the most beautiful parts of the state. Folks come from all over the country to stay at this mountain bike retreat. Among other activities are hiking along some of the best trails in north Georgia. Perhaps you may want to try local trout fishing or look for some white water adventure. Bike rentals are available for those who need them.

Find out more:
Mulberry Gap Bunkhouse and Camping
Ellijay, GA
Phone: 706-698-2865
Website: mulberrygap.com

BAY SPRINGS MOTEL AND CAMPGROUND

Stay on Weiss Lake in Centre, Alabama. They take pride in cleanliness and customer service. The rates are very reasonable. There are places for RVs and campsites for your convenience. There are many activities within driving distance. Also, there are local restaurants that offer a variety of choices. Take a scenic drive along the Lookout Mountain Parkway, or enjoy scenic views along the rim of Little River Canyon. There are many ideas that compliment a day around the area, referred to as the "Crappie Capital of the World."

Find out more:
Bay Springs Motel and Campground
Centre, AL
Phone: 256-927-3618
Website: bayspringsmotelandcampground.com

CHESTNUT BAY RESORT

In Leesburg, Alabama, you will want to consider renting a place to stay on the lake. The amenities include boat rentals, a beach area, waterslide, pools, and more. They have lake house rentals for a nice family getaway that can fit most budgets. There are plenty of things to do and places to eat within reasonable driving distance. Enjoy a visit to small towns such as Cave Spring, scenic Cedar Bluff, DeSoto Falls, and more! Noccalula Falls is a fun family thing to do if you have small kids.

Find out more:
Chestnut Bay Resort
Leesburg, AL
Phone: 256-526-7778
Website: chestnutbayresort.com

CHANTICLEER INN BED AND BREAKFAST

Stay across the street from some of the nation's oldest and popular attractions. Remember the signs that dotted the highways across the nation that said "SEE ROCK CITY"? Perhaps you have made a visit to Ruby Falls or the nation's oldest attraction, the Incline Railway? Take some time at Point Park and learn about the "Battle Above the Clouds." The views from Lookout Mountain are breathtaking, looking at the Tennessee River below the park bluff and getting a distant look across seven states!

Find out more:
Chanticleer Inn Bed and Breakfast
1300 Mockingbird Lane

Lookout Mountain, GA 30750
Phone: 706-820-2002 or 866-424-2684
Website: stayatchanticleer.com

THE LIGHTHOUSE MOTEL AND RESTAURANT

One will find some of the best dining in the area here!
Make a reservation at the motel with single adjoining
rooms for a reasonable rate. They are on Lake Weiss in
Cedar Bluff. Close to the motel there are opportunities for
fishing and boating. Plan a daytrip in any direction, such as
DeSoto Falls State Park, Tigers for Tomorrow, Noccalula
Falls, Little River Canyon, northwest Georgia attractions,
and more.

Find out more:
The Lighthouse Motel and Restaurant
Cedar Bluff, AL 35959
Phone: 256-779-8400
Website: thelighthousemotel.com

HISTORIC BANNING MILLS

The word "historic" doesn't describe the inn, you have to
see it! There is a lot of local history of the old mill that has
become a part of Georgia history, if not the nation. Both
the Civil War and the paper industry are part of its past,
worth learning about. This secluded retreat has become a
popular destination in west Georgia for anniversaries,
church retreats, business functions, and more. There is an
abundance of activities. Their canopy tree tours are a big
draw in the same area of the state.

Find out more:
Whitesburg, GA
Phone: 770-834-9149
Website: historicbanningmills.com

WOODBRIDGE INN AND RESTAURANT

The spot where the inn sits was a popular one for the
Native Americans who lived in the area. In the 1800s, folks
who came in on the stagecoach would stop here at the
Woodbridge Inn. Some would travel the crossroads and
make a stop for the night. Georgia governors and other
famous statesmen would frequent the Inn. Come for the
experience and dine in the restaurant that has been a
popular venue for years!

Find out more:
Woodbridge Inn and Restaurant
Jasper, GA 30143
Phone: 706-253-8500
Website: woodbridgeinn.net

BARNSLEY GARDENS

Listed as one of the nation's top resorts. Stay in one of the
cottages. There are a variety of activities to enjoy. There is
horseback riding, kayaking, world-class golf, and more.
Located near the historic district of quaint shops and the
local attractions offered in Bartow County and the
surrounding region. There have been folks who came by

helicopter on special occasions! They can make special moments come true!

Find out more:
Barnsley Gardens
Adairsville, GA 30103
Phone: 770-773-7480 or 877-773-2447
Website: barnsleyresort.com

SEQUATCHIE VALLEY GUEST RANCH

This unique ranch near Chattanooga brings a taste of Montana to its guests. Live on the ranch for a day or enjoy a guided trail ride along the river. If you're there on the weekend, travel to church on horseback. Check out the events during the year. This is a popular retreat for churches. Couples can celebrate an anniversary and get a taste of the midwest. Family members can saddle up and have a fun getaway to remember!

Find out more:
Sequatchie Valley Guest Ranch
Dunlap, TN
Phone: 423-554-4677
Website: TnHorseVacations.com

CALLAWAY GARDENS

Located in middle Georgia on the west side, they have been an attraction since 1952. Today they are one of the top resorts in the country that is a draw for folks all over the nation. They have first class accommodations. You can reserve one of the lodge rooms, cottages, or villas. With ten dining options, one can enjoy a variety of choices. From southern style to fine dining, there is something for every occasion and taste. Take some time to enjoy a day of golf or tennis. Find a favorite spot to fish. Go on a hiking or biking trip. Robin Lake Beach is the largest man-made sandy beach island in the world. Don't forget their seasonal events such as the "Fantasy in Lights" at Christmas.

Find out more:
Callaway Gardens
Pine Mountain, GA
Phone: 706-663-2281 or 1-800-Callaway
Website: callawaygardens.com

BRASSTOWN VALLEY RESORT AND SPA

In the north Georgia mountains, spend some time at the highest elevation in Georgia. Enjoy beautiful mountain scapes, scenic drives along country mountain roads. Along the way, you'll find Brasstown Valley Resort, filled with hundreds of acres where you can take a leisurely vacation with a variety of activities. Play a round of golf or competitive game of tennis, or lay back a fishing pole along one of the streams. Take a hike at the resort or along the Appalachian Trail. With the excursion, opportunities are almost endless! Horseback riding, rock climbing, tubing, canoeing, and guided trips are available. Go birding and see some of north Georgia's unique visitors throughout the year. Stay in one of the lodging rooms or cottages at the resort and enjoy first class amenities.

Find out more:
Brasstown Valley Resort and Spa
Young Harris, GA
Phone: 706-379-9900
Website: brasstownvalley.com

TARRER INN

A gem in southwest Georgia is located in the historic town square of Colquitt. Folks traveling through the state will reserve lodging at the Inn. It's just off the Martha Berry Highway and convenient on trips to and from the Florida coast. You may want to reserve a night to stay at the inn, with an ambience of the Victorian era. Some folks take a long side trip to dine at the Tarrer Inn. Sample fine dining featuring traditional southern cooking with a touch of elegance, sprinkled with true customer service. Fresh homemade jams and desserts are a special treat that adds a personal touch.

Find out more:
Tarrer Inn
Colquitt, GA
Phone: 229-758-2888

SEVENTY FOUR RANCH

At the ranch, one will sample a taste of the "old west" in north Georgia. This bed and breakfast offers amenities and services for every member of the family. Enjoy camping on the ranch, trail rides, old-fashioned cooking by the campfire, and more. Go horseback riding, fishing, boating, or take a leisurely walk. Check out their rooms and rocking chair front porch, hidden in the Appalachian foothills.

Find out more:
Seventy Four Ranch
Jasper, GA
Phone: 706-692-0123
Website: SeventyFourRanch.com

Host An Event Or Retreat

Family reunions, school outings, church retreats, and more southern favorites

Historic Gordon Lee Mansion in Chickamauga, Georgia

So you are responsible for finding a place for your family reunion, birthday party, business function, or church retreat. Do something different! Perhaps you would like to have a group catered picnic at the beach, or enjoy a live concert on the farm in beautiful northwest Georgia. A bit of history with a touch of "Gone with the Wind" might be right for the occasion. How about scheduling it close to a tourist town, where folks can spend a few days with their families without traveling a great distance! Maybe you are looking for a retreat center that caters to mostly ministries. Some have overnight accommodations. Here is a list that has been referred by others, for your convenience.

LEE AND GORDON'S MILLS

Settlers came to this area and resided here when the town was called Crawfish Springs. A gristmill and a general store were built and in operation by the same man when it was handed down to family, until the 1850s. It was used during the Civil War by Union and Confederate troops. In 1929, it was sold and in operation for almost forty years. Finally, it was restored by the new owner. This old mill is a historic landmark, built in the early 1800s. Today, it can be rented for special occasions. See it as it was originally, almost 200 years ago.

Find out more:
Lee and Gordon's Mills
Chickamauga, GA
Phone: 706-375-4728
Website: leeandgordonsmills.com

GORDON-LEE MANSION

This historic antebellum plantation home survived the devastation of the Civil War. Built in 1847, one may literally think of "Tara" from "Gone with the Wind." The mansion is within twenty miles south of Chattanooga, Tennessee. A cannon battle was fought on its grounds, making it part of the oldest and largest Civil War battlefield in the United States. They have seasonal events throughout the year. The mansion is also open for family reunions, church functions, business events, and more.

Find out more:
Gordon-Lee Mansion
Chickamauga, GA
Phone: 706-375-4728
Website: gordonleemansion.com

THE RAGSDALE INN

This early 19th century Victorian home offers a variety of services. They have bed and breakfast packages for guests from across the nation and world, who have come for a few days to explore the Appalachian foothills. It is like stepping back in time to a different era. This lovely home, with a gorgeous wraparound porch, was almost destroyed by developers before it was bought and restored. They offer catering services. Folks can rent the home for family reunions, church functions, business functions, weddings, and more.

Find out more:
The Ragsdale Inn
Dallas, GA
Phone: 770-443-3440
Website: theragsdaleinn.com

OAK HILL

This early 20th Century estate, built as a Greek revival style home is located on 170 acres in Floyd County, Georgia and belonged to the pioneer educator, Martha Berry. It is open for tours. There are events throughout the year that the community is invited to. The facility has sections of the home that can be rented out for meetings, family reunions, etc. The students built and gave it to Martha Berry in 1922. It is definitely a trip worth driving to see and tour.

Find out more:
Oak Hill
Mount Berry, GA
Phone: 706-368-6789
Website: berry.edu/oakhill

HIGHTOWER FALLS

The cotton gin dates back to 1832 and was built near an eighty foot cascading waterfall. In 1845, a mill was built and sheep were raised on 2,000 acres of property. During the Civil War, the Union Army camped on the property, but did not burn any of the structures. A home was built a couple of miles away in the late 1850s. It is privately owned and not open to public. After the turn of the century, folks would come to picnic near the falls. After 1972, there were more than 100 campsites, a restaurant, meeting room, stables, cabins, and a store. In 1996, it was opened as an event facility. Weddings, family gatherings, and other special occasions bring folks from all around to enjoy the falls.

Find out more:
Hightower Falls Facility
Cedartown, GA
Phone: 770-748-8588
Website: hightowerfalls.com

THE WHITLOCK INN

These lovely Victorian homes are next to each other on Whitlock Avenue near the Marietta Square. The Whitlock Inn sits on the property that was once a Marietta resort. The resort burned more than a century ago. Today, this lovely home that was built in the early 1900s offers a variety of services. For over fifteen years, this home has been a jewel in the area for family reunions, business functions, meetings, and more. Guests are also invited to reserve lodging to enjoy one of their bed and breakfast packages.

Find out more:
The Whitlock Inn
Marietta, GA
Phone: 770-428-1495
Website: whitlockinn.com

PRATER'S MILL

This historic mill was built in 1885. The Union Army camped on the site. Once a thriving mill with a blacksmith's shop and a general store, it was in operation for 95 years by the original family. Today, the Prater's Mill Foundation is the caretaker of the mill. There are events during the year. It has become a popular place in the community. The facility can be reserved for private events.

Find out more:
Prater's Mill Foundation
500 Prater Mill Road NE
Dalton, GA 30721
Phone: 706-694-6455
Website: Pratersmill.org

JOIN THE SHOW!
Rent out the local community theater for the next birthday, family reunion, or event for your organization. Contact your local performing arts production company. They usually are a not-for-profit organization and provide services to the community by providing family productions and education.

STEP BACK IN TIME

There are a number of museums that have the space to rent out for the next family or group outing. Learn about Native Americans, the space program, local history, Civil War, and a variety of other topics that could put a little twist on that special event.

RINGGOLD DEPOT

This historic depot near Chattanooga was built in 1850. Today, it is used for various annual events. It can be rented for private functions. There is significant history regarding the railway and the Civil War, as it was fought through north Georgia. There are a few shops and restaurants nearby the depot.

Find out more:
The Ringgold Depot
Ringgold, GA
Phone: 706-935-3061
Website: cityofringgold.com

CHATTANOOGA GROUP TRAIN EXCURSION

If you have a group large enough, groups may charter a special riding event for their organization. For a dynamic railway adventure, consider one of the many trips offered out of Chattanooga. From sixty minutes to six hours, take a journey around Missionary Ridge, or down the tracks across northwest Georgia to Chickamauga. Chartered trips are fun for everyone. While you are in Chattanooga, check out the museum and learn of their railroad history.

Find out more:
Tennessee Valley Railroad Museum
Chattanooga, TN
Phone: 423-894-8028
Website: tvrail.com

GRAND SLAM PARTY

Host the next event at your favorite minor league team's venue and watch them play ball. Many of the Major affiliates offer catered meals and locations in the stadiums for most any size group. It will be a big hit with the kids from 1 to 101!

Find out more:
Read the "Grand Slam" chapter for information on the closest teams to you and find out what they offer for private events.

CAMP SUNRISE

This is a unique camp in north Georgia. Camp Sunrise is a Bible based Christian ministry whose goal is to educate through planetarium programs, illustrated science lectures, and camps to develop a greater appreciation for the Creator. The gospel message is given through Bible teaching and counseling, recreational activities are offered for physical exercise and learning for students. They offer programs throughout the years and more. Their camps include Junior Camp, Teen Camp, Family Camp, and Teen Retreat. Attend one of their planetarium programs as they look at astronomy and other related subjects. Adults and youth can learn about God's creation, as related through Scripture. Ask about their outdoor educational programs for your group. The facilities are open for private use to church ministries which hold to the same doctrinal purpose of Camp Sunrise.

Find out more:
Camp Sunrise
Fairmount, GA
Phone: 706-337-2775
Website: CampSunrise.com

WOODLAND CHRISTIAN CAMP

Churches who are looking for a place to hold retreats,
camps, or other programs should consider Woodland
Christian Camp. There is a wide choice of activities,
including an eight acre lake on this 120 acre campground.
There is plenty of lodging for almost 400 campers. Meeting
rooms and dining facilities are available.

Find out more:
Woodland Christian Camp
Temple, GA
Phone: 770-562-3103
Website: Woodlandcamp.org

CAMP GIDEON

This camp is a Christian ministry based in Acworth,
Georgia. There are lodging, dining, and meeting facilities.
A number of activities are offered, such as canoeing or
paddle boating on Lake Allatoona, swimming at the beach,
fishing, a variety of outdoor sports, and more. A number of
programs are offered throughout the year. Consider
hosting a church retreat or camp of your own!

Find out more:
Camp Gideon
Acworth, GA
Phone: 770-974-7744
Website: campgideon.com

Ponderosa Bible Camp
Mentone, AL
Phone: 256-634-4397 (office)
Website: ponderosabiblecamp.com

TUCKALEECHEE RETREAT CENTER

In the Smoky Mountain National Park region, this facility is available for church retreats, business outings, family reunions and more. There are modern lodging rooms, kitchen, dining, and meeting rooms available. The mountain scape is included at no additional charge. Hiking, biking, overlooks, caverns, and more are close to the center. Convenient to Pigeon Forge and Gatlinburg.

Find out more:
Tuckaleechee Retreat Center
Townsend, TN
Phone: 865-448-6442
Website: tuckaleecheeretreatcenter.com

CAMP SKYLINE

In the Appalachian foothills along the Lookout Mountain range are some of north Alabama's most scenic areas. Camps dot the landscape, and one you may want to consider is Camp Skyline for your next church retreat or group activity. It is close to many attractions in Chattanooga, Atlanta, north Georgia mountains, and north Alabama. There are lodging facilities, meeting places, dining areas, and camp activities such as swimming in the river, horseback riding, rope courses, canoeing, and more.

Find out more:
Camp Skyline Ranch
Mentone, AL
Phone: 800-448-9279
Website: campskyline.com

CAMP RIVERVIEW
The beautiful retreat center has programs for every age. Groups from all over the Southeast use the campus or come to a scheduled retreat throughout the year. There is dining, lodging, and meeting facilities to meet the needs of the guests. Host a special retreat for your church, school, or family outing. Riverview is for everyone. Enjoy a variety of activities at the camp and in the surrounding area.

Find out more:
Camp Riverview
Mentone, AL
Phone: 256-634-4043
Website: riverviewcamp.com

ALPINE CAMP
You are looking for a retreat center for your church, school, or family group. Consider Alpine Camp! Off season is a great time to use the facility to host your event. The camp

can hold from 35 to several hundred campers. There are meeting spaces, dining areas, lodging facilities, camp activities, and attractions convenient to the retreat area.

Find out more:
Alpine Camp
Mentone, AL
Phone: 256-634-4404
Website: alpinecamp.com

COHUTTA SPRINGS CONFERENCE CENTER
Cohutta Springs offers a variety of options for both conference setting and camp facility. There are lodging facilities, kitchen and dining area, and activities to meet the needs of your group. There are local attractions within a reasonable driving distance as well. So come and enjoy a weekend retreat reunion, conference, camp, and other opportunities.

Find out more:
Cohutta Springs Conference Center
Crandall, GA
Phone: 706-695-9093
Website: cohuttasprings.com

APPALACHIAN TRIVIA
Fun for the road

Game #1

1. A bakery in Chattanooga created an original dessert known across the country. What is it?
2. Miniature golf was invented by the same man who founded what nationally known attraction?
3. The incline railway is older than the Spanish American War. True or False?
4. US 27 meanders the length of the state of Georgia and is also known by what other name?
5. A sign in Copper Harbor denotes the point at which US 41 begins in the state of _____.
6. Where is the marker that announces the end of the Great Locomotive Chase?
7. The famous Little Chapel in Ringgold, Georgia has had more than 3,000 marriages, making Ringgold known as the _____?
8. The 1996 Summer Olympics held what events at the Ocoee Whitewater Center above Blue Ridge and McCaysville, Georgia on Highway 64?

SCAVENGER HUNT THROUGH THE BOOK

1. Find the best place to host a birthday party that could be out of this world.
2. Find where there is a marker indicating the end of the Great Locomotive Chase.
3. Find a commercial cave where you can take a boat tour.

ANSWERS

TRIVIA: (1) The Moon Pie; (2) Rock City; (3) True; (4) The Martha Berry Highway; (5) Michigan; (6) Ringgold, GA; (7) Marriage Capital of the South; (8) Canoe, kayak, and slalom events
SCAVENGER HUNT: (1) Huntsville Space and Rocket Center; (2) Ringgold; (3) Lost Sea

APPALACHIAN TRIVIA
GAME # 2

DID YOU KNOW?
At one time, Georgia bordered the _____.

FAMOUS PEOPLE
Who were these famous people in the space program?
1. Wernher von Braun
2. Jan Davis
3. William McMichael Shepherd

TRIVIA

1. The oldest hotel in Alabama was in business until a few years ago in Mentone, Alabama. Which is it?
2. Coca-Cola was founded in Atlanta. Where was the site of the first bottling franchise?

3. Rock City and Ruby Falls are close to each other on Lookout Mountain, but which is actually in Georgia?
4. During the colonial times, the Tennessee River was a French trade route between _____ and _____?
5. Some say that the last battle of the Revolutionary War took place in Ohio. Others say that Lookout Mountain was the last location. What is the most likely answer?
6. What is the second largest national military park in the nation? It is the oldest _____. Highway 27 starts in _____?
7. Cohutta, Georgia is close to what Tennessee state park where they say the "Trail of Tears" began?

SCAVENGER HUNT

1. Find a place to stay that was open when "horse and buggy" was a major source of transportation.
2. Find Paula Deen's cousin's place to eat.
3. Find out the name of the person about whom there is a play and movie called "The Miracle Worker".

ANSWERS

DID YOU KNOW: Mississippi River
FAMOUS PEOPLE FROM THE SPACE PROGRAM: (1) Physicist (Huntsville, AL); (2) Astronaut (Huntsville, AL); (3) Astronaut (Oak Ridge, TN)

TRIVIA: (1) Mentone Springs Hotel; (2) Chattanooga; (3) Rock City; (4) Mississippi Valley and Charleston, South Carolina; (5) Neither; some still say the last battle fought was during the Battle of 1812, referred to as the Second Revolutionary War; (6) Chickamauga and Chattanooga National Military Park; (7) Interstate 69 in Fort Wayne, Indiana; (8) Red Clay State Historic Park
SCAVENGER HUNT: (1) Woodbridge Inn, Jasper, Georgia; (2) Gabriel's Desserts, Marietta, Georgia; (3) Helen Keller

APPALACHIAN TRIVIA
Game #3

DID YOU KNOW?
The Smoky Mountains in Tennessee connect to the
_____ in _____?

FAMOUS PEOPLE
Do you remember these sitcoms? Gomer Pyle, USMC and The Andy Griffith Show. What characters did the following actors play?

1. Frank Sutton
2. Jim Nabors
3. George Lindsey

TRIVIA

1. The Union Army fought through the night and lost which battle? They lost more than three times than the Confederates and were delayed for a week.
2. What is on display in the Bessemer, Alabama?
3. The world's largest space and rocket center is located where?
4. Haralson County, Georgia has recently developed their _____.
5. What is the name of the Cherokee newspaper that was published in New Echota and is still in print in another location, almost 200 years after the "Trail of Tears?"
6. Who created the Cherokee alphabet and had most Native Americans reading within a month?
7. The Silver Comet Trail crosses ninety miles and three Georgia counties before it crosses the Alabama state line. There is a railroad tunnel one must enter to complete the journey. How long is the tunnel?
8. "Georgia's oldest bookstore" is located in Carrollton, Georgia. There are only two older than it in the South. The name of the bookstore is

   _____.

SCAVENGER HUNT

1. Find the oldest symphony in the South.
2. Find a place where there is a mysterious wall that is more than 800 feet long.

ANSWERS

DID YOU KNOW? Fannin County, Georgia
FAMOUS PEOPLE: (1) Sgt. Carter, Actor, Clarksville, Tennessee; (2) Gomer Pyle, Actor, Sylacauga, Alabama; (3) Goober, Actor, Jasper, Alabama
TRIVIA: (1) Pickett's Mill, in Dallas, Georgia; (2) Hitler's typewriter; (3) Huntsville, Alabama; (4) quilt trail; (5) The Cherokee Phoenix; (6) Sequoyah; (7) 500 feet, the Silver Comet Trail travels 90 miles from Cobb County, Paulding County, and Polk County; (Horton's Books)
SCAVENGER HUNT: (1) Rome Symphony; (2) Fort Mountain State Park

APPALACHIAN TRIVIA
GAME # 4

DID YOU KNOW?
The triple region of Georgia, Alabama, and Tennessee has the largest _____ in the country, if not the world?

FAMOUS PEOPLE
Do you know where these famous people lived?
1. Jeff Foxworthy
2. Oliver Hardy
3. Winston Groom
4. Nell Carter

TRIVIA

1. What was the name of the bridge built in 1890 that crosses the Tennessee River and is in use today, and is also referred to as the "world's longest pedestrian bridge"?

2. Chief John Ross was born in Cherokee County, Alabama. Name the town.

3. Highway 27 and Highway 41 ends in what Florida city?

4. Fannin County is bordered by the states of Tennessee and North Carolina. Almost 50% of the county's land is in the

   _____.

5. In the early 1900s along Route 41 in north Georgia, one could see bedspreads hanging for sale mile after mile. What did some nickname this route?

6. When Georgia was a new colony, Route 41 was actually referred to as _____. It eventually connected with Spanish-controlled Florida.

7. The Creek Indian word for Lookout Mountain is

   _____.

8. How deep is Carters Lake?

SCAVENGER HUNT

1. Find a place where you can sit for hours and watch trains go by.

2. Find a trail where the major piece of equipment you will need is your camera. You may see a bald eagle!

3. Find a place that hosted the 1996 Summer Olympics kayak competition.

ANSWERS

DID YOU KNOW: Number of caves
FAMOUS PEOPLE: Atlanta, Georgia; (2) Harlem, Georgia; (3) Fairhope (author of "Forrest Gump); (4) Birmingham, Alabama (actress and singer)
TRIVIA: (1) The Walnut Street Bridge, Chattanooga, Tennessee; (2) Turkey Town; (3) Miami; (4) Chattahoochee National Forest; (5) Peacock Alley; (6) The Old Spanish Trail; (7) Chattanooga; (8) 450 feet deep
SCAVENGER HUNT: (1) Dalton Welcome Center; (2) North Alabama Bird Trail; (3) Ocoee Whitewater Center

APPALACHIAN TRIVIA
GAME #5

DID YOU KNOW?
The name of the road that is listed as one of the nation's most scenic byways that continues ninety miles from Gadsden, Alabama to Chattanooga, Tennessee is

_____.

FAMOUS PEOPLE
Where are these famous TV personalities from?
1. Alton Brown
2. Nancy Grace

TRIVIA

1. In 1836 what state was the first to declare Christmas as a legal holiday?

2. Which one of these athletes were not from Alabama: Hank Aaron, Bo Jackson, Joe Louis, Willie Mays or Jesse Owens?

3. Cave Spring has the second largest pool in the state and the only one shaped like

_____.

4. The man who played in several movies and provided the voice of "Winnie the Pooh" was from Cedartown, Georgia. What is his name?

5. The cabin on Berry College campus is named after which one of its visitors?

6. In Douglas County, Georgia, in Sweetwater State Park, one can see ruins of an old town called

_____.

7. The oldest town in Alabama was _____. There, Andrew Jackson was a tailor's apprentice. Every other year there is a festival, walking tours, and living history.

8. The town of Ross Landing along the Tennessee River was named after the Cherokee Chief, John Ross. What would the name later be changed to?

SCAVENGER HUNT

1. Find the cafe with a name that represents a train stop.

2. Find the highest peak in the Appalachian Mountains in Alabama.

ANSWERS

DID YOU KNOW: The Lookout Mountain Parkway
FAMOUS PEOPLE: (1) Marietta, Georgia (Food Network
TV Personality); (2) Macon Georgia (TV Personality)
TRIVIA: (1) Alabama; (2) They all lived in Alabama at one
time; (3) Georgia; (4) Sterling Holloway; (5) President
Theodore Roosevelt; (6) Manchester; (7) Mooresville; (8)
Chattanooga
SCAVENGER HUNT: (1) The Whistle Stop, Kennesaw,
Georgia; (2) Cheaha State Park

YOUR VOTE COUNTS!

Have you explored the Southwestern part of the Appalachian region? This includes northern parts of Georgia, Alabama, and Mississippi. Don't forget rare gems at the tip of North Carolina, South Carolina and east Tennessee. While we will take most suggestions in the Appalachian region, tell us about unique places nearby for us to share with others.

1. World's largest:_____
2. Best Tour _____
3. Best Excursion: _____
4. Favorite Southern Inspiration _____
5. Most fun place to volunteer: _____
6. This little town had some really neat shops_____
7. We attend a great community play at: _____
8. Best Restaurant worth the drive_____
9. We found a nice place to stay at:_____
10. Most interesting event facility: _____
11. Great place to hold a church retreat: _____
12. Best idea on a budget: _____

PLEASE INCLUDE LOCATION WITH EVERY ONE OF YOUR ANSWERS.
Send to: D. Jay Powell, P.O. Box 603, Hiram, GA 30141

ABOUT THE AUTHOR

D. Jay Powell is a freelance travel writer who resides in the Appalachian foothills, where the Smoky Mountains meet the Blue Ridge Mountains as they meander through the top of Georgia. His writings have been published in a variety of local community magazines and newspapers, as he writes about the treasures in the beautiful region where he grew up, as well as the surrounding states. He has spoken on such subjects as "how to put together an itinerary" at local seminars. He assists churches with information to help plan their outings, and families to help make the most of their time together. He shares with his readers the many exciting things in their own backyard. The love for travel writing came as he began to research the Christian heritage in his own region. As he began to find an abundance of information, he discovered adventure around every turn. He believes that this is a place where great memories can be made. The opportunities are endless for every occasion!
Contact information:
D. Jay Powell
Phone: 770-723-6574
Email daytripgetaways@gmail.com
Website: DayTripGetAways.com

Favorite Spots: Coldwater Creek is near Oxford, Alabama. Locals wade on a hot, sunny day. However, it represents the Jordan River in the lives of my family members. After coming to know Christ, some family members in years past had an old fashioned riverside baptism at a place along the creek. As the author of this book, I try to stop here each year to give thanks to the Lord on my way to the Southern Christian Writers Conference.

Made in the USA
Columbia, SC
04 May 2023

16067793R00083